Indian Education System and Different Standards

Author

Dr. Neetu Yadv

Published By

Indian Education System and Different Standards

ISBN 978-93-83459-19-3

Author

Dr. Neetu Yadv

Lucknow, UP

Published by

Bonfring
292/2, 5th Street Extension, Gandhipuram,
Coimbatore-641 012. Tamilnadu, India.
E-mail: info@bonfring.org
Website: www.bonfring.org
Contact: 0422 3928700

Acknowledgement

I am overwhelmed with joy, and avail this opportunity, to express my deepest gratitude and sincere regards to people who in one way or the other have helped me throughout the year 2012 to complete my work successfully. The present work would not have come into existence without their altruistic contributions and efforts.

It gives me immense pleasure to express my deep sense of gratitude to my parents, for timely advice and perennial encouragement throughout the course of my work.

I also deeply acknowledge the unflinching support, motivation and constant encouragement of my friends whose inspiration constantly helped me a lot in finalizing this project.

Dr. Neetu Yadv
Lucknow UP

PREFACE

India, with more than a billion residents, has the second largest education system in the world (after China). Experts estimate that 32 percent of its current population is under the age of 15. But counter to the image of India as a youthful engine of economic growth where many urban based citizens work in some of the best technology- centered jobs in the world, males in India complete just 2.9 years of schooling on average, female just 1.8 years. And for the small proportion who do persist through primary and secondary schooling, the quality of instruction varies widely, depending on the region of the country and whether one is enrolled in a state support public school or a fee- based private school.

Despite the highly inefficient delivery of public services, high levels of teacher absenteeism and non teaching activity, many Indian students remain motivated to succeed on the college entrance exams. The high level of competition for entry into the Indian Institutes of Technology, the Indian Institutes of Management and other top institutions is enough to spur millions of students to achieve at remarkably high levels, particularly in the areas of science and mathematics. The increased demand for higher education is not currently being met: only ten percent of the age cohort is actually enrolled in higher education. But in a country with such a large population, ten percent enrolment amounts to 0 million students, resulting in 2.5 million new college graduates a year. These numbers driven by the private sector opportunities abroad, and increasingly, back in India will continue to ensure India's prowess in delivering high quality technical manpower.

<table>
<tr><th>Unit</th><th>Contents</th><th>Page No</th></tr>
</table>

Unit I

1.1 ADMINISTRATION OF EDUCATION

The central and the state governments have joint responsibility for education, with freedom for the state governments to organise education within the national framework of education. Educational policy planning is under the overall charge of the central Ministry of Human Resource Development which includes the Department of Elementary Education and Literacy and the Department of Secondary and Higher Education. The Ministry is guided by the Central Advisory Board of Education (CABE) which is the national level advisory body. The education ministers of all the different states are members of the board.

The National Council of Education Research and Training (NCERT) (1961) defines the National Frame Curriculum for classes I - XII. It also functions as a resource centre in the field of school development and teacher education. State Councils of Educational Research and Training (SCERT) are the principal research and development institutions in all the states. At secondary level, school boards at state level affiliate schools and set examination standards in accordance with the national framework. The Central Board of Secondary Education (CBSE) and Council for Indian School Certificate Examinations (CISCE) cover all India besides the National Institute of Open Schooling (NIOS).

1.2 NATIONAL POLICY ON GENERAL EDUCATION

Under the national constitution, education was a state matter until 1976. The central government could only provide guidance to the states on policy issues. In 1976 the constitution was amended to include education on the concurrent list. The initial attempts of designing a National Education Policy were made in 1968 but it was only in 1986 that India as a whole had a uniform National Policy on Education. The National Policy on Education 1986, modified in 1992, defines the major goals for elementary education as universal access and enrolment, universal retention of children up to 14 years and substantial improvement in the quality of education. The National Policy of Education of 1992 also aims at vocationalisation of secondary education and greater use of educational technology.

The policy has been accompanied by several programmes such as the District Primary Education Program (DPEP) launched in 1994 and the National Campaign for Education for All (Sarva Shiksha Abhiyan) launched in 2001/2. A proposed bill on the right to education (draft, November 2005) stresses the right of all children from age 6 until their 15th birthday to receive elementary education either in school or non-formal education (NFE).

The Indian government is preparing the universalisation of secondary education (USE). The main aim is to provide high quality secondary education to all Indian adolescents up to the age of 16 by 2015, and senior secondary education up to the age of 18 by 2020

Crucial problems in India are teacher absenteeism, noted by UNESCO in 2005; high teacher pupil ratios; and inadequate teaching materials and facilities, particularly in rural areas.

At the other end of the scale, children attending urban schools, especially middle and upper class children in private schools, are subjected to extreme competition from a very early age in order to qualify for admission into the best schools.

in 1979-80, the government of india, department of education launched a programme of non-formal education (nfe) for children of 6-14 years age group, who cannot join regular schools - drop-outs, working children, children from areas without easy access to schools etc. the initial focus of the scheme was on ten educationally backward states. later, it was extended to urban slums, and hilly, tribal and desert areas in other states.

1.3 SCHOOL EDUCATION

A uniform structure of school education, the 10+2 system, has been adopted by all the states and Union Territories (UTs) of India following the National Policy on Education of 1986. Elementary school, Class I – VIII, is recognised as the period of compulsory schooling, with the Constitutional amendment making education a fundamental right. A majority of the states and Union Territories (UTs) have introduced free education in classes I-XII. In states/UTs where education is not free for classes IX and above, the annual fee varies considerably.

The pre-school covers two to three years. The elementary stage consists of a primary stage comprising Classes I-V (in some states I-IV), followed by a middle stage of education comprising Classes VI -VIII (in some states V-VIII or VI -VII). The minimum age for admission to Class I of the primary school is generally 5+ or 6+. The secondary stage consists of Classes IX-X (in some states VIII-X), and a senior secondary stage of schooling comprising classes XI-XII in all states. In some states/UTs these classes are attached to universities/colleges. The number of working days of school education in a year is generally more than 200 days in all the states/UTs.

1.4 PARTICIPATION IN PRIMARY AND SECONDARY EDUCATION

The Gross Enrolment Ratio (GER), which indicates the number of children actually enrolled in elementary schools as a proportion of child population in the 6-14 years age group, has increased progressively since 1950-51, rising from 32.1% to 82.5% in 2002-03, according to statistics published by the Ministry of Human Resource Development in India.

The rate of increase in GER of girls has been higher than that of boys. The dropout rate at the primary level (Classes I-V) declined from 39% in 2001-02 to 34.9% in 2002-03. However the GER only covers 61% of children from classes VI to VIII.

In 2002/3 the dropout rate was estimated at 34.9% at the end of lower primary classes and 52.8% at the end of upper primary. The dropout rate was 62.6% at the end of secondary school (Class X). There are wide disparities among the different states in the number of children completing primary and secondary school from less than 20% to more than 80%, according to the central statistics from the Ministry of Human Resource Development.

1.5 NATIONAL CURRICULA

The National Council of Education Research and Training (NCERT) formulated the first Curriculum Framework in 1975 as a recommendation to the individual states. NCERT was accorded the responsibility of developing a binding National Curriculum Framework through the National Policy on Education (NPE) (1986).

NCERT reviews the curriculum every five years on the basis of consultations within the whole school sector. The core areas of the curriculum are common. Teaching of English is usually compulsory in classes VI-X in most of the states/UTs.

NCERT published a New National Curriculum framework in 2005. The New National Curriculum will be introduced in textbooks in three phases:

- Phase one, 2006-07: classes I, III, VI, IX and XI.
- Phase two, 2007-08: classes II, IV, VII, X and XII
- Phase three, 2008-09: classes V and VIII

NCERT has gradually been changing the curriculum from traditional information provision to be more learner-oriented and competence-based.

1.6 NATIONAL CURRICULUM FRAMEWORK 2000

The National Curriculum Framework 2000 operates with the concept of the Minimum Levels of Learning (MLLs) identifying certain essential levels of learning for each stage of school education.

PRE-PRIMARY EDUCATION

The National Policy on Education defines the objective of early childhood care and education (ECCE) as being the total development of children in the age group 0-6 years. Early Childhood Education (ECE) or pre-primary education (2 years), part of the ECCE, shall prepare children for school.

Teaching at this stage, according to the National Curriculum Framework, comprises group activities, play–way techniques, language games, number games and activities directed at promoting socialisation and environmental awareness among children. Formal teaching of subjects and reading and writing are prohibited. However, NCERT strongly criticised the actual pre-school programmes for exposing children to structured formal learning, often in English with tests and homework, in the introductory notes to the new National Curriculum Framework 2005.

The competition for the best education starts at a very early age. Newspapers from September 2005 in India report of tremendous pressure on three-year old children being prepared by their parents for nursery interviews and competing with a huge number of other children for places in the most prestigious private pre-schools. The newspapers report on private persons/institutes that offer help to parents in preparing their children for nursery interviews. Other

PRIMARY EDUCATION

At the primary stage, emphasis is on the process of understanding, thinking and internalising. The National Curriculum contains the following subjects:

Subject	Lower primary Classes I-II	Lower primary Classes III-V	Upper primary Classes VI-VIII
Language(s)	The mother tongue/regional language	The mother tongue/regional language	Three Languages — the mother tongue/the regional language, a modern Indian language and English
Art education - -			All kind of creative activities including the child's own creations

Mathematics	Woven around the world of the learner	Integrated approach	Essentials of mathematics for every day activities, including geometry
Art of healthy and productive living	Creative education, health and physical education, work education, value inculcation		Integrated approach to music, dance, drama, drawing and painting, puppetry, health and physical education, games and sports, yoga and productive work
Environmental		Experiences to	

studies		help socio emotional and cultural development with a realistic awareness and perception of phenomena occurring in the environment	
Health and physical education			- Games and sports, yoga, NCC and scouting and guiding
Science and technology			Key concepts across all the disciplines of science, local and global concerns
Social sciences			Social, political

			and Economic situation of India and the world, including Indian cultural heritage. Academic skills social skills and civic competencies
Work education			Agricultural and technological processes including participation in work situation

Source: National Curriculum Framework 2000

In all language education programmes, the stress is placed on the ability to use the language in speech and in writing for academic purposes, at the workplace and in society in general.

The duration of a class period may be around 40 minutes and, according to NCERT, the school year should be a minimum of 180 days, and "…A primary school should function for five hours a day out of which four hours may be set aside for instruction. For the upper primary and secondary schools, the duration of a school day should be six hours out of which five hours should be kept for instruction and the rest for the other routine activities."

SECONDARY EDUCATION (2 YEARS, GRADES IX-X)

In grades IX-X the scheme of studies should include the following subjects: three languages (the mother tongue/the regional language, a modern Indian language and English), mathematics, science and technology, social sciences, work education, art education, health and physical education. Foreign languages such as Chinese, Japanese, Russian, French, German, Arabic, Persian and Spanish may be offered as additional options. The curriculum in mathematics should take into account both the learning requirement of learners who will leave school for working life, and of students who will pursue higher education.

According to the NECRT Secondary School Curriculum 2002-2004 (Vol. 1, Main Subjects) the suggested number of weekly periods per subject in grade X is as follows:

Subject	Suggested number of periods in grade X
Language I	7
Language II	6
Mathematics	7
Science and technology	9
Work education or pre-vocational education	3 + 2 to 6 periods outside school hours
Social science	9
Art education	2

The boards, however, according to NCERT, often offer limited or no optional courses: two languages (one of which is English), mathematics, science and social sciences are the typical examination subjects. A few boards encourage students to choose an optional course from a range that includes economics, music and cookery.

HIGHER SECONDARY/SENIOR SECONDARY EDUCATION (2 YEARS, GRADES XI–XII)

The curriculum at this stage is divided into an academic stream and a vocational stream.

ACADEMIC STREAM

The objectives of academic courses are to promote problem-solving abilities and convey higher levels of knowledge. The curriculum at this stage comprises foundation courses and elective courses. Foundation courses consist of (i) language and literature, (ii) work education, and (iii) health and physical education, games and sports.

The study of language prepares a student to both learn and use language in the classroom, the community and the workplace. The choice of the language to be studied is decided by the learner. Work education includes e.g. developmental projects in a village or city. Generic Vocational Courses (GVC) aim at developing employment-related generic skills regardless of the persons' occupations. The student should choose three elective courses out of the subjects prescribed by the boards. Elective courses may include bridging courses between the academic and vocational streams.

The list of courses may include modern Indian languages, Sanskrit, classical European languages and their literatures, English (academic and specialised), other foreign languages, subjects in the sciences and mathematics, computer science, accountancy, business studies, engineering, political science, history, sociology, psychology, philosophy, fine arts and others.

NCERT prescribes that courses should be listed together without dividing them into mutually exclusive groups. Nonetheless, several boards restrict the combinations in the form of a 'science stream', 'arts stream' and 'commerce stream'. Some schools tailor their classes to medical and engineering courses. Universities restrict admissions based on the subjects and combinations of courses studied in the +2 stage. Sixty percent of the instructional time is devoted to the instruction of elective subjects and forty percent to the foundation course.

The introduction of the vocational stream was recommended by the central Kothari Commission (1964-66). The National Policy on Education, 1986 (revised 1992) set a target of twenty-five percent of higher secondary students in vocational courses by 1995. So far, enrolment is far below this.

The courses for the vocational stream consist of:

- A language course
- A general foundation course
- Health and physical education, and
- Elective vocational courses

Vocational education covers areas like agriculture, engineering and technology (including information and communication technology), business and commerce, home science, health and para-medical services and humanities.

Language courses are organised to cover the grammatical structures and additional vocabulary particular to the trade or vocation. The general foundation course for the vocational stream comprises general studies, entrepreneurship development, environmental education, rural development and information and communication technology.

Vocational electives are organised according to employment opportunities. Practical training is an essential component of the vocational courses, according to the National Curriculum Framework, with seventy percent of time devoted to vocational courses. The certificate issued should mention the competencies acquired and the credits earned.

ORGANISATION

The organisation of teaching is based either on an annual or semester system. In most cases, a year's course is divided into two parts to be covered in the two halves of an academic session in the annual system. Marks are accorded to a certain number of periods; the total mark is an average of marks accorded to the different parts of curriculum in an annual or semestrial examination (e.g. a paper corresponding to a 3-hour written examination).

The example below copied from the Senior School Curriculum 2007 (Central Board of Secondary Education) illustrates a typical curriculum (in history) and the maximum marks accorded to the different parts of the curriculum.

In the semester system, recommended by NCERT, students take a number of credit hours corresponding to their requirements and capacity, and at their own pace. However, only a few institutions have adopted the semester and credit system.

1.7 NATIONAL CURRICULUM FRAMEWORK 2005

The National Curriculum Framework 2005 points out the need for plurality and flexibility within education while maintaining the standards of education in order to cover a growing variety of children. The Framework recommends that learning shifts away from rote methods and that the curriculum reduces and updates textbooks. Peace education is included as a dimension in education. The new curriculum proposes a broader spectrum of optional subjects, including the revalorisation of vocational options. Courses may be designed to offer optional modules, rather than trying to cover everything and overfilling courses too much.

The National Curriculum Framework 2005 also proposes changes within the examination system (examinations for classes X and XII) allowing reasoning and creative abilities to replace memorisation. The children should be able to opt for different levels of attainment.

TEXTBOOKS

Most states have legislated to create bodies for the preparation of syllabi and textbooks. The states have established various mechanisms for the preparation and approval of textual materials.

However, a study in 2005, undertaken by the Central Advisory Board of Education (CABE), of textbooks used in government schools (not following the CBSE syllabus) and in nongovernment schools (including social and religious schools) showed that many textbooks reinforce inequalities and neglect rural, tribal or female realities.

According to NCERT' Newsletter, in 2005, CABE proposed the institution of a National Textbook Council to monitor textbooks.

EXAMINATION AND ASSESSMENT

In all the states and Union Territories, public examinations are conducted at the end of classes X and XII by the respective State Boards of Secondary and Higher Secondary Education.

Ministry of Human Resource Development has published a list of recognised state boards for secondary and higher secondary education.

The minimum age for admittance to the Secondary School Examination generally varies from 14+ to 16+. The minimum age for Higher Secondary School Examinations varies from 16+ to 18+ years. Some states/UTs do not have an age restriction.

The Central Board of Secondary Education (CBSE), established by a special resolution of the Government of India in 1929, prescribes examination conditions and the conduct of public examinations at the end of Standard X and XII.

The Council for the Indian School Certificate Examinations (CISCE), Delhi, was established in 1958 by the University of Cambridge, Local Examinations Syndicate as a self-financing national examination board. The Council conducts the Indian Certificate of Secondary Education (Standard X) and the Indian School Certificate (Standard XII) examinations.

CISCE affiliates schools using English as a medium of instruction. The title of the final qualification varies depending upon the examining body. The titles used by the central examining boards are:

CBSE

- All India Secondary School Certificate (Standard X).
- All India Senior School Certificate (Standard XII).

CISCE

- Indian Certificate of Secondary Education (ICSE Standard X).
- Indian School Certificate (ISC Standard XII).
- Certificate of Vocational Education (CVE XII).

CENTRAL BOARD OF SECONDARY EDUCATION

Central Board of Secondary Education (CBSE) is one of the three national boards of secondary education in India. CBSE has affiliated around 8,300 schools including government and independent schools. It also affiliates schools in some 20 African and Asian countries. About 200 new schools are affiliated each year. Study teams conduct regular inspections of the affiliated institutions. CBSE has a central office and 6 regional offices. Permanent affiliation is obtained after a number of years. Affiliation is granted according to strict criteria. A list of affiliated schools can be found on CBSE' s website: http://www.cbse.nic.in.

Information from the procedure of the All India Senior School Certificate (Standard XII) (extract):

The Board conducts examination in all subjects except General Studies, Work Experience, Physical and Health Education, which will be assessed internally by the schools based on cumulative records of student's periodical achievements and progress during the year.

In all subjects examined by the Board, a student will be given one paper each carrying 100 marks for 3 hours. However, in subjects requiring practical examination, there will be a theory paper and a practical examination as required in the syllabi and courses.

A candidate may offer an additional subject that can be either a language at elective level or another elective subject as prescribed in the Scheme of Studies, subject to the conditions laid down in the Pass Criteria.

A candidate will get the Pass Certificate of the Board, if he/she gets a grade higher than E in all subjects of internal assessment unless he/she is exempted. Failing this, result of the external examination will be withheld but not for a period of more than one year.

In order to be declared as having passed the examination, a candidate shall obtain a grade higher than E (i.e. at least 33% marks) in all the five subjects of external examination in the main or at the compartmental examinations.

The pass marks in each subject of external examination shall be 33%. In case of a subject involving practical work a candidate must obtain 33% marks in theory and 33% marks in practical separately in addition to 33% marks in aggregate in order to qualify in that subject.

A candidate failing in two of the five subjects of external examination shall be placed in compartment in those subjects provided he/she qualifies in all the subjects of internal assessment.

A candidate who has failed in the examination in the first attempt shall be required, to re-appear in all the subjects at the subsequent annual examination of the Board.

A candidate who has passed the Senior School Certificate Examination of the Board may offer an additional subject as a private candidate provided the additional subject is provided in the Scheme of Studies and is offered within six years of passing the examination of the Board.

A candidate who has passed an examination of the Board may reappear for improvement of performance in one or more subject(s) in the main examination in the succeeding year only; however, a candidate who has passed an examination of the Board under Vocational Scheme may reappear for improvement of performance in one or more subject{s) in the main examination in the succeeding year or in the following year provided he/she has not pursued higher studies in the mean time. He /she will appear as private candidate.

Candidates who appear for improvement of performance will be issued only Statement of Marks reflecting the marks of the main examination as well as those of the improvement examination.

The major objective is to prescribe conditions of examinations and conduct public examinations at the end of Classes X and XII and to grant certificates to successful candidates of the affiliated schools. All affiliated schools follow the national scheme of 10+2.

Here is an example of testimonial for All India Senior School Certificate Examination from 2000:

CBSE is regulated but not financed by the central government. Financing is assured by fees from the affiliated schools. CBSE accepts private candidates. CBSE develops its curriculum on the basis of the national curriculum framework. The curriculum is revised every 5 to 10 years. Two of the front line curriculum subjects are revised every year.

According to CBSE, it strives notably to adapt current teaching methods and content of teaching to an innovative and creative society in the form of subjects such as functional English, bio-technology, entrepreneurship, life skills education, and disaster management. An important objective is the distressing of education, including no homework or examinations in grades I and II and only achievement reports in grades III-V.

Information technology is compulsory in grades IX +X. Language studies include a possible 27 different languages besides Hindi and English. One teacher may teach four subjects up to grade X. The board uses the term learner (for student) with emphasis on the learner's role in learning. Two subjects undergo a performance analysis (marks, questions, learning) each year to cope with poor performance.

Examination is monitored and organised to avoid fraud. CBSE issues duplicates of certificates under certain conditions. CBSE also organises in-service training of teachers and special programmes for new principals.

GRADING

Both Standard X and XII are normally marked on a percentage basis. The minimum passmark varies depending upon the subject. According to the UK NARIC, the following marking scheme is used in most states for the Standard XII examinations, in comparison with that used by the central boards.

Percentages	Performance assessment	CBSE	CISCE
85%+, 80-85%, 70-80%	Excellent, Superior, Very good	A1-A2, B1	One, two, three
60% - 70%	Good	B2	Four
50% - 60%	Satisfactory	C1	Five
40% - 50%	Average	C2	Six
35% - 40%	Pass	D	seven

DOCUMENTS

The pass-document is issued by the relevant Board of Secondary Education. It shows the type of programme (academic or vocational), the subjects passed and the marks obtained out of total marks as well as the aggregate marks, percentage obtained, and result as well as the overall grade/division.

NATIONAL INSTITUTE OF OPEN SCHOOLING (NIOS)

National Institute of Open Schooling (previously known as the National Open School) was established in November 1989 as an autonomous registered society. The institute provides basic programs such as secondary education courses and senior secondary education courses on an open education basis.

NIOS conducts examinations twice a year and candidates can appear in one, two or more subjects. Credits are accumulated until the certification criteria are fulfilled. NIOS has at its disposal a network of accredited study centres all over India providing support to learners.

ISLAMIC EDUCATION

India also has a system of Islamic education. Several different sects have their own schools where they teach Islamic subjects and Arabic to mainly (but not only) Muslim children. A Madras as Modernization Programme was introduced in the National Policy on Education of 1986 and in the updated plan of 1992.

Some Indian states have established government Madras as Education Boards with which madras as can be affiliated. Selected madras as receive government support to teach secular "modern" subjects such as science, mathematics, English and social sciences.

A number of Indian universities recognise credentials from certain madras as thus enabling their graduates to continue to higher education. Students typically go on to study Arabic, Urdu, Persian and Islamic subjects but also other subjects.

Unit II

VOCATIONAL AND TECHNICAL EDUCATION AND TRAINING

2.1 EDUCATION AND TRAINING OF THE INDIAN LABOR FORCE

According to the report "Industrial Training Institutes of India: The efficiency study report" published by the International Labour Organisation (ILO) in 2003, the educational levels of the labour force in India are rather low. About 44% of all workers were illiterate, while 22.7% had completed primary school in 1999. About 33.2% of the labour force graduated from the middle school. This share is higher in urban areas, at 57.4%.

Only 5% of the young Indian labour force (20-24 years) had received formal vocational training compared to 60% to 80% in industrialised countries.

The ILO report characterises the technical education and vocational training system in India as a three-tier system:

- Certificate-level craftsmen and women trained in Industrial Training Institutes (ITIs)/Industrial Training Centres (ITCs) (craftsmen Training Scheme) as well as through formal apprenticeships as semi-skilled and skilled workers.

- Diploma-level graduates trained in polytechnics as technicians and supervisors.

- Graduate and post-graduate level specialists (e.g. ITIs, engineering colleges) trained as engineers and technologists.

As described already, higher secondary education incorporates a vocational stream. There are around 17 ministries/departments that provide or finance vocational education and training programmes. Some of the courses are conducted in formal institutions with uniform curricula and prescribed examination standards while others are needs-based courses. In India, technical education refers to the field of study rather than the level, so technical education includes disciplines such as engineering, management etc. at undergraduate and postgraduate level, as well as diploma programmes in technical fields. Vocational education normally refers to vocational programs at school and higher education level, while vocational training refers to trade/craft education.

This chapter describes vocational training and technical education at certificate craft and technician levels, while qualifications at graduate and post-graduate higher level are described in Chapter 3. Vocational education at secondary level is described in Chapter 1.

2.2 POLICY AND COORDINATION

The Joint Council of Vocational Education (JCVE) is responsible for the overall co-ordination of all other bodies and departments concerned with vocational education. The State Council of Vocational Education (SCVE) is a body with similar functions to JCVE at the state level. The District Vocational Education Committees perform the function of local co-ordination.

The All India Council of Technical Education (AICTE) is a statutory body which regulates engineering and technology, management and technician education throughout the country at the national level. AICTE covers programmes of technical education including training and research in engineering, technology, architecture, town planning, management, pharmacy, applied arts and crafts, hotel management and catering technology etc. at different levels. However, most of the programmes accredited are at diploma or BTech/Bachelor level with few accredited programmes at technician level (polytechnics), see page xxxxx.

The National Council of Education Research and Training (NCERT) and many of the State Council of Education Research and Training (SCERT) have a division devoted to vocational education for research and development.

2.3 TRAINING OF SCHOOL LEAVERS AT GRADE VIII/PLUS

There are six ministries/departments offering programmes with a total annual training capacity of about 1,271,000. The Directorate General, Employment and Training (DGE&T), Ministry of Labour, supervises the biggest training system (about 60%) followed by the Ministry of Human Resource Development (HRD) with about 40%.

Annual vocational training capacity of ministries/departments in India

Ministry/Department	Estimated training capacity/persons trained (annually)
Min. Health and Family Welfare	20,000 persons
Min. Human Resource Development	
Vocationalization of Secondary Education	490,000 persons
Apprenticeship training	19,000 persons
National Institute of Open Schooling	7,000 persons
Dept Information technology	
DOEACC O-level	75,000 persons
Min. Labour (DGET)	
Apprenticeship Training Scheme	About 500,000 persons
Craftsmen Training Scheme	About 150,000 persons
Other long-term Training Scheme	7,000 persons
Dept Small Scale Industries	2,000 persons
Dept Tourism (Food Crafts Institutes)	1,000 persons
Total	1,270,000 persons

Source: ILO, 2003, page 7

ADMINISTRATION

Two tripartite bodies, the Central Apprenticeship Council (CAC), a statutory body, and the National Council of Vocational Training (NCVT), a non-statutory body, operate as advisory institutions. There is a proposal to merge NCVT and CAC into a new apex body by establishing an All India Council for Vocational Training.

The NCVT was set up by the Government of India in 1956. It is chaired by the Minister of Labour with members representing central and state government departments as well as the labour market organisations, the professional bodies and the underprivileged castes and women in India.

NCVT awards National Trade Certificates in engineering, building, textile and leather trades and prescribes standards for syllabi, space, duration of courses and methods of training, recognises training institutions and organises trade tests. State Councils for Vocational Training (SCVTs) advise the state governments on training policy matters.

2.4 PRINCIPAL TRAINING SCHEMES

CRAFTSMEN TRAINING SCHEME (CTS)

The Craftsmen Training Scheme (CTS) was introduced in 1950 by the Indian Government. The scheme is addressed at young people from 14 to 25 years old. The scheme takes place under the auspices of the Directorate of Vocational Education and Training (DVET) at state level.

CTS include training programmes in around 49 engineering and 49 non-engineering trades. The period of training varies from 6 month to three years.

About 70% of the training period is practical training and the rest theoretical (trade theory, workshop calculation and science, engineering drawing, social studies including environmental science and family welfare).

National qualifications have been developed by NCVT and are periodically revised to keep pace with new technology in industry. The qualifications mainly concern basic industrial trades. Non-engineering trades such as agro-processing, personal and community services, insurance and financial services in the fast growing sectors are not represented, according to the ILO report from 2003. ILO has pointed out that there are few national vocational qualifications available for women. However, women have a high participation in services sectors with few training possibilities.

Few states use the possibility to develop their own vocational qualifications and issue awards by the State Councils for Vocational Training (SCVTs) because those qualifications are not recognised nationally.

Training takes place at either central or state government Industrial Training Institutes (ITIs) or private Industrial Training Centres (ITCs) approved by the state government and affiliated to NCVT. There are about 4,650 public and private training institutes in India.

All India Trade Tests for Craftsmen are conducted by the DGE&T, Ministry of Labour, under the aegis of the National Council for Vocational Training in July (main) and January (supplementary) every year. Successful candidates are awarded the National Trade Certificate and classified as semi-skilled craftsmen.

A National Trade Certificate is a recognised qualification for recruitment to posts in Central/State Government establishments. The different Craftsmen Training Scheme programmes can be found on the website of the Directorate General of Employment and Training (DGE&T)/Ministry of Labour. Please see http://dget.nic.in/schemes/cts/welcome.htm

THE APPRENTICESHIP TRAINING SCHEME (ATS)

The Apprenticeship Training Scheme (ATS) is regulated under the Apprentices Act, 1961. Employers in specified industries shall engage apprentices at ratios prescribed for a designated trade. In 2002, the total apprentice capacity was nearly 216,000 with actual utilisation being around 155,000. The duration of training ranges from six months to four years.

The apprentices gain practical knowledge in shop floor training in industrial establishments and theoretical instructions in Government Related Instruction Centres.

An apprentice should be at least 14 years old. The minimum educational qualification is different for different trades. Currently, according to information on the website of the Ministry of Labour, there are 138 trades in 31 trade groups. Qualifications vary from Standard VIII pass to XII pass (10+2) system. Please see http://dget.nic.in/schemes/ats/welcome.htm

Apprentices may be so-called fresher's (no previous vocational qualification) or graduates of a Craftsmen Training Scheme.

Apprentices without a basic vocational qualification shall undergo basic training.

Basic training and related instructions are conducted in Basic Training Centres (BTCs) or Related Instruction Centres (RICs). The Industrial Training Institutes (ITIs) are also used as Basic Training Centres for the Apprenticeship Training programmes. A curriculum is prescribed for each trade. Apprentices take the All India Trade Test of Apprentices conducted by the National Council of Vocational Training (NCVT). Successful apprentices are awarded the National Apprenticeship Certificate by the Central Apprenticeship Council and classified as skilled workers.

There are also Graduate Apprenticeships for engineering graduates and Technician Apprenticeships for diploma holders from polytechnics (established in 1974) and Technician (Vocational) Apprenticeships for the graduates of higher secondary vocational courses. There are 101 subject fields that have been designated for the category of Graduate & Technician apprenticeships. 94 subject fields have been designated for the category of Technician (Vocational) apprenticeships.

CRAFTS INSTRUCTOR TRAINING

There are six Central Training Institutes for training of Instructors under the Directorate General of Employment & Training (Ministry of Labour). These institutes conduct regular, refresher and retraining programs for the craft instructors in engineering and non-engineering trades. Please see the list at http://dget.nic.in/schemes/cits/welcome.htm.

PRIVATE INDUSTRIAL SCHOOLS AT STATE LEVEL

Private industrial schools function at state level. Training is offered in the areas such as catering, tailoring, computer software, beauty culture, and office automation, besides engineering and non-engineering trades. The training period varies from 45 days to two to three years. Candidates are admitted from 8th standard to Secondary School Leaving Certificate (SSLC) (passed/failed). Examination is conducted at state level and certificates are issued to the successful candidates by State Government.

ADVANCED VOCATIONAL TRAINING SCHEME AND HI-TECH SCHEME

In order to upgrade and update the skills of industrial workers, an Advanced Vocational Training Scheme (AVTS) was established in 1977 by DGE&T, Ministry of Labour in collaboration with United Nations Development Programme (UNDP)/ILO. The training scheme takes place at 6 Advanced Training Institutes (ATIs) under DGE&T and 16 Industrial Training Institutes (ITIs) of 15 State Governments.

The objective of the Hi-tech scheme is to produce trained personnel within electronics, computers and modern production systems.

2.5 TECHNICIAN EDUCATION

Polytechnics typically offer one to three year sub-degree diploma courses in all subjects except medicine. Polytechnics are widely spread over all the states and Union Territories and are affiliated to the respective State Boards of Technical Education. The latter set the levels and standards of the courses and organise the system of evaluation by examination. Currently there are over 1,200 polytechnics in India. Polytechnic diplomas are awarded by the State Boards.

Polytechnics in India are designed traditionally to focus on 'supervised technician' training programmes, although an increasing number of polytechnics have begun to offer courses leading to degrees. The training is mostly institutional (with some industrial experience), the curricula predominantly theory oriented, and the location mostly urban.

Most three- to four-year Diploma courses require a Standard X pass as the entry qualification, with the exception of Higher National Diploma courses that require Standard XII passes.

Polytechnics also provide Post-graduate Certificate/Diploma courses in various subjects on both full-time and part-time bases. Since course titles, duration and entry qualifications vary from state to state, care is needed in evaluating these types of credentials. AICTE is trying to streamline the nomenclature for this type of qualification.

Unit III

3.1 GENERAL CHARACTERISTICS

Higher education is on the concurrent list in the Indian constitution, meaning that it is a shared responsibility between the Union or Central Government and the State Governments. The Department of Secondary and Higher Education is placed within the Ministry of Human Resource Development. There is also a Department of Education in each state.

The Central Government is responsible for the major policy on higher education and for the co-ordination and determination of standards in higher education institutions. State Governments for their part are responsible for the establishment of state universities and colleges and for providing grants for their development and maintenance.

As mentioned in Chapter 1, the Central Advisory Board of Education (CABE) coordinates the work of the Union and the States in the field of education. The Union Government has established regulatory and statutory bodies to discharge their responsibilities. A list of these bodies and their mandates can be found in Appendix 1.

Higher education institutions are funded by the Central Government through the University Grants Commission (UGC), one of the statutory bodies, or by the State Governments. The UGC allocates and disburses maintenance and development grants to all Central universities and to all colleges affiliated to Delhi and Banaras Hindu University as well as to some nominated universities. Other institutions may receive support from different development schemes of the UGC.

State universities and colleges are funded by the respective states. There are also some other sources of funding. Self-financed or private universities are not common in India although many colleges are financed by non-governmental sources.

Only universities established or incorporated by or under a Central Act, Provincial Act or State Act, an institution deemed to be a University under Section 3 of the University Grants Commission Act or an institution specially empowered by an Act of Parliament have the right to confer degrees in India.

The University Grants Commission (UGC) specifies the nomenclature of degrees with the approval of the Central Government and publishes a list of all the degrees on the UGC's website. Some of these are oriental degrees, for example Shashtri (B.A.) and Shiksha Shashtri (B.Ed). The UGC also specifies the minimum standards for instruction; see Appendix 2. The relevant regulatory bodies prescribe the norms for the granting of degrees within their respective subject areas.

3.2 Education Reforms in the Recent Years

The policy of the government is to bring about improvement in information infrastructure and develop quality education through Information and Communication Technology (ICT) integration in the higher education institutions in the country.

The vocationalisation of undergraduate education has been on the agenda since the Eighth Plan of 1994/95 but it is still a burning question. The university sector is experiencing undue pressure on the system for postgraduate education. The UGC is therefore encouraging the introduction of skill-oriented courses at universities. This will enable the graduate to possess a basic degree as well as a professional qualification, thus hopefully making it easier to find employment in the wage sector or to go into self-employment.

> *The UGC only recently decided that students should be allowed to take two degrees or a degree and a certificate/diploma in parallel. They gave examples of such double degrees: - a student may pursue a Bachelor's degree in history along with a diploma in tourism or science journalism.*
>
> *According to the UGC, only the best students would be fit to take on this heavy burden of studying different subjects in parallel. The numbers would therefore be quite limited. - Another possibility mentioned by the UGC is to continue from certificate to diploma and even up to bachelor level by adding an extra year of studies.*

The UGC has introduced an introductory course on environmental studies that is compulsory for undergraduate courses of all branches. The UGC has also launched several other programmes in order to modernise the higher education sector.

For example, a custom nationwide communication network named UGC-Infonet has been set up. An E-Subscription initiative has also been set up to provide HE institutions with access to 9,000 journals with full text through gateway portal access. Furthermore, a Consortium of Education Communication has been established to provide education to students across the country via electronic media.

3.3 FRAMEWORK OF HIGHER EDUCATION

India has one of the largest education systems in the world and also one of the most complex.

The European system of higher education was introduced in India by the British in 1857 with the establishment of universities for European education in three cities and withdrawal of support for indigenous education. At the time of independence, there were 20 universities and 500 colleges in India but the number has increased rapidly since then and the student enrolment has gone up by nearly 36 times.

The present-day educational structure in India consists of:

- Central universities 18,
- State universities 211,
- Institutions deemed to be universities 99,
- Institutions established under State Legislature Act 5,
- Institutions of National Importance 13, Colleges 17,625.

There are, in addition, 51 Academic Staff Colleges for academic training of teachers. These numbers are changing as new institutions are established; the number of colleges in particular is continuously growing.

3.4 THE STUDENT POPULATION

The enrolment rate is 7% and a majority of the students, 89%, were enrolled at undergraduate level in the year 2003/04. 9% were enrolled at master level and less than 1% were doing research. Another 1% were on diploma or certificate courses.

Enrolment of students in higher education institutions was 9.6 million, closer to the GER of 9% during 2002-3. With 43,000 teachers and a pupil-teacher ratio of 22:1, the higher education sector in India is continuing to grow. Added to this is the 420,000 enrolment in polytechnic institutes and 760,000 enrolment in open universities, giving an approximate total enrolment of 11 million.

An additional 87,000 Indian students were studying in foreign universities in 2001-02 and around 8,000 international students, notably from Asia and Africa, were studying in Indian universities in 2002-03. 43% of all international tertiary level students in the OECD area are from Asia. Indian students constitute 4% of the group. Presently, international students from about 125 countries are pursuing various undergraduate, postgraduate and research programs in India at recognised universities and institutions.

In the year 2003/4, the distribution across faculties was:

- 45% of students enrolled in arts faculties,
- 20% of students enrolled in science faculties,
- 18% of students enrolled in faculties of commerce/management,
- 17% of students enrolled in professional faculties.

This is also reflected in the conditions of admission; it is relatively easy to gain admission to non-professional colleges (except for some selected colleges in large cities), while it is much more difficult to get a place at a professional college, e.g. in medicine, engineering, pharmacy etc. Admission to professional colleges is generally based on separate admission tests. The fees charged differ between subjects. Accordingly, it is more costly to study in a professional college.

3.5 INSTITUTIONAL STRUCTURE

Under the constitutional provision, central and state governments establish multi-faculty conventional universities. These are of both unitary and affiliating types. Nearly 50% of universities in India belong to this category.

There are also professional universities such as technical, medical, law and agricultural universities. These are established by state governments and are also of unitary and affiliating types. The third category is open universities established by central and state governments. These offer open and flexible education through distance learning using correspondence courses/modern educational technology such as interactive TV, etc.

DEEMED TO BE UNIVERSITIES

Section 3 of the UGC Act provides that an institution of higher education, other than a university, which is doing work of a very high standard in a specific area can be declared as an institution deemed to be a university. The practice of establishing 'deemed to be universities' in the private/joint sector began in 1986. The University Grants Commission (UGC) has the power to recommend that an institution should have the status of a 'deemed to be a university'. The Central Government makes the decision. Such institutions enjoy the academic status and privileges of a university and are able to strengthen activities in the field of their specialisation, rather than becoming a multi-faculty university of the general type. A 'deemed to be university' can not have affiliated colleges.

Apart from Universities and Deemed to be Universities, there are also some institutions offering professional Under Graduate (UG), Post Graduate (PG) and research programmes established as Centres of Excellence, some by an Act of Parliament, such as the Indian Institute of Technology (IIT) and others by the Central Government such as the National Law Institutes, National Institute of Design, Indian Institute of Management, National Institute of Fashion Technology, etc.

AFFILIATED COLLEGES

Affiliated colleges can be either publicly funded (governmental colleges), partly funded by the government or private self-financed colleges. They are affiliated to a university. Most affiliated colleges offer first-degree courses, but some are approved by the university to offer postgraduate courses as well. The university prescribes the curricula, controls the examinations and awards the degrees. The role of the colleges is to prepare students for the examinations of the university. For example, Hindu College in New Delhi, one of 80 affiliated colleges to Delhi University, is regulated under the Act of the University:

"College means an institution maintained or admitted to its privileges by the University and includes an Affiliated College and a Constituent College;

Explanation I. 'Affiliated College' means an institution recognised by the University in accordance with the provisions of this Act and the Statutes in which instruction is provided in accordance with the provisions of the Statutes and Ordinances up to the Bachelor's degree, but exclusive of Honours and Post-graduate degrees;"

CONSTITUENT COLLEGES

During the 1950s a distinction developed between constituent and affiliated colleges. Constituent colleges were normally situated on or closer to the university campus. They generally have a stronger association with the university than the more remote affiliated colleges, and are generally regarded as offering a more consistent standard of education than in the affiliated system.

AUTONOMOUS COLLEGES

Autonomous colleges are a recent development. The system of autonomous colleges was introduced in the early 1980s. They aim for higher standards and greater creativity than the affiliated colleges. The University Grants Commission's (UGC) National Policy on Education (NPE) 1992 says about autonomous colleges: "The objective of granting autonomy to certain colleges is to provide academic freedom, especially in designing their curricula; evolving new methods of teaching, research and learning; framing rules for admission; prescribing courses of study; setting examination papers and conducting examinations."

The autonomous colleges are still part of a university but have some autonomy in determining curricula, teaching methods and assessment as mentioned above. An autonomous college has its own Governing Body, academic council and a Board of Studies for each subject. Their degrees are awarded by the parent university with the name of the college mentioned on the diploma. The scheme of marks is issued by the college.

According to UGC guidelines, the right of autonomy is not conferred indefinitely. The right must be continually assessed and earned. In 1999 there were a total number of 123 autonomous colleges affiliated to 28 universities spread over eight states.

Autonomous status enables the colleges to offer more postgraduate diplomas using the faculty and facilities already available. According to one institution quoted in the Pier World Education Series on India, an advantage of autonomous status is: "After introduction of autonomy, we are able to observe a tremendous boost in the morale of the students and an improvement in their performances, both in curricular as well as extra-curricular activities."

Many autonomous colleges, at least at the postgraduate level, have changed their academic calendar to the semester system, and the grading pattern has changed from the percentage of marks system to letter grades.

Every college in India is affiliated to a university; either as an affiliated college, a constituent college or an autonomous college. The UG C tends to prefer the development of autonomous colleges.

3.6 HIGHER EDUCATION OUTSIDE THE UNIVERSITY SECTOR

Institutions outside the purview of the universities can award other types of qualifications that might be recognised for employment or for further studies at universities.

The Association of Indian Universities (AIU) is an inter-university organisation with the aim to share information and facilitate co-ordination between Indian universities as well as between universities and the government. AIU maintains a list of institutions whose postgraduate diplomas in management have been equated with an MBA degree. This list contains 32 institutions and includes, among others, the prestigious Indian Institutes of Management.

The AIU examines proposals received from institutions that have been approved by the All India Council for Technical Education (AICTE) and grant them academic equivalence. According to their yearbook for the year 2004, 4 institutions were considered. Of these, 3 were granted equivalence after inspection by the AIU visiting Committee.

Higher education is also carried out at different professional institutions in the fields of accounting, engineering and computer science.

Some courses are offered by universities as well as by other institutions outside the university system. An example is within architecture where the degree Bachelor of Architecture is given by universities and the Diploma of Architecture by other providers than those within the university sector.

3.7 PRIVATE HIGHER EDUCATION INSTITUTIONS

A bill on the establishing of private universities, The Private Universities (Establishment and Regulation) Bill, was introduced in the Rajya Sabha (Council of States) of the IndianParliament in 1995. The bill is still pending. Some states have introduced laws on private universities and there are a handful of private universities in India. A law in the state of Chhattisgarh opened up for the mushrooming of private universities in that state but that particular law has been overruled by the Indian Supreme Court and the universities have thereby been declared illegal.

India offers a typical example of how private initiatives come to be encouraged in developing countries. When the country became independent in 1947, there was a dearth of educated and skilled workers to undertake the massive nation-building activities and the national government virtually "nationalised" all the then existing private higher education institutions and commenced funding them directly. These institutions have come to be known as grant-in aid institutions as against government-run public universities and colleges.

By the late 1980s, the number of colleges increased from 500 to about 5,000. By then, the resources of the government reached their limit and most of the state governments were forced to stop establishing or funding new colleges. Therefore, the government encouraged the private initiatives without any commitment for financial support, with a stipulation that they should function under the academic regulations of the universities in that area. This resulted in the emergence of a new category of private institutions which are run with student fees without financial support from the government.

According to WES, this new crop of private initiatives locally called "self-financing" institutions now outnumber the public ones in some states, more so in the southern states of India. The policy of the government is to encourage privatisation without giving room for commercialisation. While such private initiatives are encouraged at the college level, there has been reluctance in accepting the concept of private universities. There are various reasons for this, the most important among them being the vociferous objection from a section of the public.

The increasing number of deemed-to-be universities is a good example of this development of the private higher education institutions in India. Most of them were originally either private higher education institutions or affiliated colleges. In order to become a Deemed-to-be university, a private institution has to fulfil the following two requirements: 1). It has existed for 5 years, 2). Inspection from the UGC or the state government has been conducted. If a private higher education institution is granted the title "Deemed-to-be university", it cannot establish its own affiliated colleges.

In 2003, the UGC enacted regulations on private higher education institutions, "UGC (Establishment of and Maintenance of Standards in Private Universities) Regulations." These regulations place the responsibility of establishing a private higher education institution on the state government and lay down clear requirements regarding establishment and recognition of private universities.

3.8 ADMISSION REQUIREMENTS

Admission to higher education is accorded on the basis of the results in the Higher Secondary School Certificate (HSSC). Entrance exams, possibly followed by an interview, take place for entrance to the Indian Institutes of Technology, professional higher education, certain centrally sponsored institutes and universities.

Admission to the most prestigious higher education institutions is highly competitive. Thus, the All India Pre-Medical Test (AIPMT) conducted by the Central Board of Secondary Education (CBSE), is taken by more than 200,000 students annually, of whom only around two thousand are accepted. Similarly, of about 200,000 students sitting the Joint Entrance Examination (JEE) to the Indian Institutes of Technology (IITs) only 4,000 are admitted.

The system of entrance tests is criticized for undermining higher secondary education. Students concentrate on their preparation for the entrance tests and neglect their studies at school. In addition, India has experienced a mushrooming of coaching institutes preparing the students for the entrance tests.

In order to give more importance to school education, the IITs have increased the required minimum score from 2006 to 60% marks in aggregate in the board examination at class XII. Furthermore students will be allowed only two attempts to pass the JEE test from 2006.

In order to reduce the multiplicity of entrance tests and the burden on applicants, separate tests conducted by each institute have been replaced by an All India Engineering, Architecture/Planning and Pharmacy Entrance Examination (AIEEE) for admission to undergraduate programmes in engineering, architecture/planning and pharmacy since 2004/5.

The states hold their own common entrance tests for admission to institutions within their states. A certain number of places are reserved for applicants from scheduled tribes and castes.

3.9 DEGREE STRUCTURE – CONTENT AND GRADING SYSTEM

India has a three-tier degree structure with bachelor, master and research degrees.

Apart from degree programmes, universities also offer shorter programs at certificate and diploma-level.

Diploma courses are available at undergraduate and postgraduate level. At undergraduate level, they vary from one to three years in length; postgraduate diplomas are normally awarded after one year's study.

There follows a description of the different degrees, and some comments on the postgraduate diploma.

3.10 UNDERGRADUATE LEVEL – BACHELOR

The standard pattern for a bachelor degree used to be two years of full-time study following 10 years of schooling and two years of intermediate study. The two-year bachelor degree was offered at some universities in West Bengal up to 1999/2000, but it was gradually phased out in the other states starting in the 1960s. The present system is commonly referred to as the 10+2+3 pattern, requiring 3 years of study for a bachelor degree in arts, science and commerce.

The professional bachelor's degrees in engineering and technology, veterinary science, and pharmacy and agriculture are obtained after 4 years of study. Architecture and medicine take 5 and 5½ years respectively. Some universities offer a 5-year integrated professional degree in law.

Bachelor degrees are awarded as Pass/General or as Honours/Special degrees. There is no common nomenclature in India and the requirements for Honours/Special degrees vary. An honours degree might require some additional papers or a separate course with specialisation in the honours subject.

Postgraduate Bachelor degrees require a bachelor for admission. Examples are Bachelor of Education, Bachelor of Library Science and Bachelor of Laws. BEd and BLibSc are one-year degrees although there is a proposition to expand the BEd to two years. LLB is a three-year degree.

Here is an example of a Bachelor degree certificate issued by the University of Madras in 2000:

3.11 POSTGRADUATE LEVEL - MASTER

Master degrees are of different types. The Master of Arts, Science or Commerce takes another 2 years of studies in the same subject after the bachelor degree. Most programmes consist of coursework although some universities have programmes involving research. The specialised master degrees, i.e. Master of Education, Master of Business Administration and Master of Computer Science, have different entry requirements. For instance, the MBA requires a bachelor's degree in any subject.

The professional master degrees are of 3 or 4 semester duration based on a 4-year bachelor in the same field. The Master of Technology and Master of Engineering take 1.5 years but there is also a 2-year Master of Science of Engineering degree by research. In medicine, the programmes last two or three years.

In some areas, such as in the engineering field, there is an entrance test for admission to master programmes. Entry is otherwise based on marks for scheduled tribes and castes and the requirements are normally 5% lower.

The integrated master degree is not necessarily a postgraduate degree; it can be a combination of two fields at undergraduate level.

The possibility of studying a new subject at master level differs. For instance, at some of the schools at Jawaharlal Nehru University, it may be possible to study for a master degree in a subject different from subjects in the bachelor degree. However, this is not a common scenario.

The postgraduate diplomas are generally shorter, with less depth and more practical work than the corresponding master's degree.

MASTER OF PHILOSOPHY

Some universities offer the Master of Philosophy (MPhil), a pre-doctoral research programme requiring a master for admission. It can either be completely research based or also include course work. The duration varies. Some institutions require the MPhil for admission to PhD programs. At the Indira Gandhi National Open University, the MPhil is not required but, without it, the student must take some extra courses. At Jawaharlal Nehru University, a student with good results from the MPhil courses can skip the thesis and continue directly to doctoral level studies.

RESEARCH DEGREES - PHD

The degree of Doctor of Philosophy is awarded at least 2 years after the MPhil or at least 3 years after the Master's Degree. It involves original research resulting in the writing of a thesis and in some cases also substantial coursework. Admission requires a Master' Degree or a Master of Philosophy in the same subject, and some universities require research experience. Students are expected to write a substantial thesis based on original research.

Some research institutes and laboratories are recognised for doctoral work although the usual case is that a university awards the degree. The Indian Institute of Science in Bangalore was the first institution to introduce an integrated.

Master-PhD programme with direct entry from bachelor level. One effect of this programme is that the student can obtain the degree approximately six months earlier than would otherwise have been the case.

CONTENT OF DEGREE PROGRAMMERS

The higher education system in India is perceived as quite rigid, a view expressed by some of the people the delegation met during the visit. For instance, it is not easy for students to transfer from one university (in India or abroad) to another, as the institutions tend not to accept studies conducted at other institutions. One factor behind this is that the annual system is still the most widely used at Indian universities. The semester system is used, but to a lesser extent.

At Jamia Hamdard, a deemed-to-be university specialising in traditional Indian Unani medicine and professional courses mostly in health-related subjects, the delegation were told that the university accepts transfer students from some colleges. Hindu College, a college of the University of Delhi, does not ordinarily admit students into the second year of an Honours course, and the rules for migration from other colleges of the same university states that a student must have a mark of at least 60% in the university examination from the previous year.

A typical bachelor degree requires English, an Indian language and two or three other subjects. The UGC has published model curricula in 38 different subjects on their website, from anthropology to zoology, that universities are free to use if they wish, in their entirety or for inspiration when determining their own syllabi.

EXAMPLES OF PROGRAMMERS OF BACHELOR'S DEGREE

An example of a typical programme of Bachelor of Arts, the B.A. programme at Hindu College of University of Delhi:

First year: two language courses (English, Hindi, Sanskrit), two discipline courses (economics, history, political science, Sanskrit, philosophy) Second year: one language, one foundation course, and two discipline courses continuing from first year Third year: one language, two discipline courses continuing from first and second year, one application course.

For the honours courses, the student would take one major course along with concurrent courses. If the main subject were English, the concurrent courses would be Hindi or Sanskrit and one interdisciplinary course.

Here are two more examples of the structure of undergraduate programmes, this time from the UGC Model Curriculum for Commerce. The first is the B.Com and the second is one of five speciality programmes

Bachelor of Commerce   **Bachelor of Accounting and Finance**

First year   Business Communication   Business Communication

Mathematics   Mathematics

Financial Accounting   Financial Accounting

Business Regulatory Framework   Business Regulatory Framework

Business Economics   Business Economics

Business Environment   Business Environment

Second year   Corporate Accounting   Corporate Accounting

Company Law   Company Law

Business Statistics   Business Statistics

Cost Accounting   Cost Accounting

Principles in Business Management   Principles in Business Management

Income Tax   Income Tax

Fundamentals of Entrepreneurship   Fundamentals of Entrepreneurship

Third year   Info Tech. and its implications in Business   Info Tech. and its implications in Business

The UGC describes the B.Com degree as a general first-degree programme offered by almost all colleges. The UGC wants to retain the professional character of education in commerce and, apart from the B.Com, they also suggest 5 speciality programmes in Accounting and Finance (BAF), Marketing (BM), International Business (BIB), Banking and Insurance (BBI) and E-commerce (B.Ec).

As can be seen, there is a high degree of communality in the course structure of the different programmes. These programmes are designed to be terminal in the sense that the graduates should be able to find jobs in lower and middle level supervisory positions. At the same time, the student should have the chance to join any of the commerce-related master programmes at a later stage in his or her career

3.12 GRADING SYSTEM

The majority of Indian institutions use a percentage system. Most Bachelor and Master Degrees are classified into divisions or classes according to the marks obtained. Grading systems vary from university to university. The Indian system is low marking, with a pass mark sometimes as low as 33% and 60% representing First Class or Division. Minimum and maximum pass marks vary. The main systems are:

Percentage system		or:	Seven Point Scale (recommended by the Association of Indian Universities)*	
First Division or Class with Distinction	70% or 75% or above		O	Outstanding
First Division or Class	60% and above		A	Very Good
			B	Good
Second Division or Class	45% (or 48% or 50%) – 59%		C	Average
			D	Below Average
			E	Poor
Third Pass Division or Class	33% (or 36% or 40%) – 44% (or 47% or 49%)		F	Very poor

*O and A correspond to the First Division or Class, Band C corresponds to the Second Division or Class.

CLASSIFICATION VARIATIONS

- Some degrees are normally awarded without classification. These include research degrees: PhD, MPhil and other general Master degrees with a research component (now rare). Master degrees in professional disciplines are often awarded unclassified. Postgraduate degrees in medicine and surgery are also normally unclassified and most universities award the MBBS unclassified; again there are exceptions.

- At some universities, students who repeat a subject are classified in the Pass Division, whatever their marks. Marks obtained are available on the marks sheet.

- On some degree certificates, the classification mentions two (or three parts). Part I (or Parts I and II) usually refer to compulsory language studies such as English and Hindi, or a regional language, while Part II (or Part III) refers to the major areas of study.

AGRICULTURAL UNIVERSITIES

According to NOOSR (2005), these universities mostly use various grade point systems.

Initially, the preferred system was a four-point scale:

- Excellent 4 points
- Good 3 points

- Fair 2 points

- Poor 1 point

For admission to postgraduate programmes a minimum mark is normally specified. This varies considerably, according to the university. One common cut-off is 2.60, but other universities require 2.00, 2.20 or 2.25. Top institutions require 3.00 on the 4 point scale.

Increasingly, agricultural universities are using a 10 point scale. The system varies considerably, and it is difficult to find information about pass marks or classification equivalence.

For example:

First Division or Class	8.50-10.00
Second Division or Class	7.00- 8.49
(no Third or Pass Division or Class)	

Admission to postgraduate programmes at a highly competitive university may require an overall grade point average (OGPA) of 7. At other universities, this cut-off point falls between 6.00 and 6.70 (a few institutions using 5.5). This may suggest that from 5.5 to 6.70 qualify for the Second Division or Class at these universities.

Other systems include a 3 point system and a 5 point system. Some agricultural universities restrict classification in the First Division or Class to graduates who complete the program within the minimum prescribed period of study, with no failures.

NATIONAL INSTITUTE OF TECHNOLOGY (NIT)/INDIAN INSTITUTES OF TECHNOLOGY (IIT)

Recent changes: Regional Engineering Colleges (REC), are now known as National Institute of Technology (NIT).

The grading system varies from the different institutions. Two examples are given below:

Grade	Grade points
A	10
B	8
C	6
D	Fail

or:

Grade	Grade Points*
S	10
A	9
B	8
C	7
D	6
E	5
F	0 Fail
W	0 (Failure due to insufficient attendance)
I	0 (Grade to be awarded later)

***In this type of grading system, the grades of first class, second class etc. are not used.**

The following is the grading scale from some universities where they state percentages. The grading system varies from university to university:

- Distinction: 75% and above
- First Division: 60% and above but less than 75%
- Second Division: 50% and above but less than 60%
- Third Division: 40% and above but less than 50%

TECHNICAL HIGHER EDUCATION

Technical education includes professional education from sub-degree level to postgraduate level. In this section, only technical education at tertiary level will be discussed. The statutory body for technical education is the All India Council for Technical Education (AICTE).

AICTE decides on norms and standards for courses, curricula, facilities, teaching staff, assessment and examination. These norms and standards are the minimum requirements to gain recognition under the AICTE Act. The National Board of Accreditation (NBA) of AICTE also uses these norms and standards in the accreditation process.

Education in the technical field is conducted at polytechnics, universities, Indian Institutes of Technology, Regional Engineering Colleges etc. The Regional Engineering Colleges are academically affiliated to universities and have a national intake. Some of them have been upgraded to deemed-to-be university status lately and changed their name to National Institute of Technology.

The polytechnics train technicians and offer courses in engineering, technology and in a few non-technological fields. These courses have already been described but some comments will be made here. Most of the Diploma courses of the polytechnics require 10 years of schooling for admission. It is possible to come across students admitted after 10+2 since those who fail to gain admission to a university may opt for a diploma at a polytechnic. Some courses, however, actually require 10+2 for admission.

The polytechnics also offer Post-Diploma Courses for working diploma holders and Advanced Diplomas in emerging fields, also for the working diploma holders. These courses may also be offered to students holding a bachelor's degree.

Polytechnics are affiliated to a State Board of Technical Education that lays down the standards for courses and evaluation.

Since course titles, duration and entry qualifications vary from state to state, AICTE has been trying to streamline the nomenclature for this type of qualification. Apart from setting norms and standards for technician education, AICTE also set norms and standards for degree programmes in engineering/technology (degrees), management education (MBA and post-graduate diplomas in management), architecture (degree or equivalent), town and country planning (undergraduate and postgraduate) and hotel management and catering technology (diploma and degree). The norms and standards can be found at the website of AICTE: http://www.aicte.ernet.in

Since many of the students pursuing further education in the Nordic countries do so in the field of engineering, the program structure prescribed by AICTE for the engineering degree program follows:

DISTANCE LEARNING – OPEN UNIVERSITIES

Since its inception in 1962 at the University of Delhi, distance education has grown considerably. There are now some sixty Institutes/Directorates of distance education attached to conventional universities and ten Open Universities, including Indira Gandhi National Open University (IGNOU) with over 150 regional centres throughout India.

Distance education programs cover about one hundred Degree/Diploma courses. Many conventional universities offer correspondence courses at their Correspondence Course Institutes (CCI). These courses are sometimes supplemented by contact classes.

IGNOU is also a national level apex body for distance education. The Distance Education Council (DEC) has been established as a statutory authority under the IGNOU Act. The DEC is responsible for the promotion, coordination and maintenance of standards of open and distance education systems in India.

The subject materials to be included in a four-year degree program in engineering need to be sub-divided as follows:

1 GENERAL 5-10%

It will be desirable to have a minimum of one course in each of the areas as below:

- Language/Communication skills
- Humanities and Social Sciences
- Economics and Principles of Management
- NSS, NCC, NSO, Rural Development

All these courses should cover the basics only. Advanced courses if considered desirable should be offered from the time allotted in professional courses. For students deficient in English language, special courses should be provided outside the normal contact time.

2 BASIC SCIENCE 15-25%

It will be desirable to have a minimum of one course in each of the following areas:

- Computer Literacy with Numerical Analysis
- Mathematics
- Physics
- Chemistry

Institutions may strengthen their curricula with common additional courses required by them as per their need to make up a maximum to 25% of the contact time available.

3 ENGINEERING SCIENCES AND TECHNICAL ARTS 15-25%

It will be desirable to have a minimum of one course in each of the following areas:

- Engineering graphics
- Workshop Practice
- Engineering Mechanics
- Electrical Science I (Basic Electrical Engineering)
- Thermodynamics and Heat Transfer
- Material Science and Engineering
- Electrical Science II (Electronics and Instrumentation)

It is also suggested that courses like (1) Engineering Systems Design (2) Building Materials (3) Surveying (4) Transport Phenomena may also form a part of this core curriculum.

4 PROFESSIONAL SUBJECTS 55-65%

Each engineering discipline will have its own minimum number of core courses. The rest of the courses will cover professional subjects as per list suggested by experts, in line with the academic regulations of the institution. Wherever possible, about 10% electives should be made available to the students. Open interdisciplinary electives allow a student to diversify his/her spectrum of knowledge. Accordingly, it is desirable that these electives be also chosen from outside the main discipline. In order to create a variety of individual skill and profile, it will be desirable to have a provision for some audit (non-credit) courses during the last two years of the degree program.

In the case of laboratory practical's a bank of experiments should be prepared, and every year new experiments/modifications should be introduced. A majority of experiments should preferably be open-ended. The students are expected to work by themselves without the aid of technicians.

Educational programs offered by IGNOU include areas in humanities, social sciences, sciences, applied sciences, computer applications, rural development, health sciences, management, education, engineering and technology.

The instruction system used by IGNOU is considered a "multi-media approach in instruction". It includes self-instructional printed course-material packages, assignments and feedbacks, supporting audio-video programming, face-to-face interaction with academic counsellors at Study Centres, practicals (laboratories) at designated institutions, project work in social programs, telecast of video programs on the National Network of Doordarskar, and broadcast of audio programmes by All India Radio (on selected stations).

Examples of the degrees awarded through distance education are B.A., B.Sc., B.Com., B.B.A., LL.B., B.Ed., B.E., B.Tech., B.Lib.Sc., M.A., M.Sc., M.Com., M.Ed., and M.B.A. degrees. Postgraduate diplomas are offered in such subjects as Business Administration, Computer Application/Systems and Management, Material Management, Pre-School Education, Statistics, and Tourism/Hotel Management.

OPEN UNIVERSITIES

- Indira Gandhi National University (1985)
- Dr. B.R. Ambedkar Open University (1982)
- Kota Open University (1987)
- Nalanda Open University (1987)
- Yashwantrao Chevan Maharashtra Open University (1989)

- Madhya Pradesh Bhoj (Open) University (1991)

- Dr. Babasaheb Ambedkar Open University (1994)

- Karnataka State Open University (1996)

- Netaji Subhas Open University (1997)

- U.P. Rajarshi Tandon Open Universities.

Unit IV

TEACHER TRAINING

Elementary teachers are trained in Teacher Training Institutes (TTI, also called Junior Basic Training Institutes or Primary Teacher Colleges) attached to State and university departments of education. The course usually lasts for two years and leads to a Diploma in Teacher Education or a Primary Teacher Certificate, P.T.C.

Secondary teachers are required to hold a Bachelor's degree in Education or in a few instances a Bachelor of Teaching. The B.ED or B.T requires one year of fulltime study following a Bachelor degree, normally in arts, science, or commerce. Teachers at the upper secondary level normally are required to hold a master's degree in their area of teaching specialization. Four Regional Colleges of Education offer a combined four-year integrated programme leading to a Bachelor's degree.

Teachers at colleges of education must hold a M.Ed. and a Ph.D. Studies for these are undertaken at a number of universities.

Level of teachers	Class-level to teach	Degree/certificates	Admission qualification	Duration	Institutions
Lower primary school teachers	Grades I to V	Diploma in teacher education, Teacher Training Certificate or Primary Teacher Certificate (P.T.C.)	10 years (SSC/Class/ Standard X)	1-2 years	Teacher Training Institutes
Upper primary school teachers	Grades VI to VIII		12 years (H.S.S.C.)	2 years	
Lower secondary level school teachers	Grades IX and X	B. Ed., Bachelor of Education degree	Bachelor	1 year	Postgraduate course at a university
Upper secondary level school teachers	Grades XI and XII		Master's degree	1 years	Postgraduate course at a university
Secondary level school teachers	Grades IX to XII	B.A. B.Ed. or BS B.Ed or BCom. B.Ed.	12 years (H.S.S.C.)	4 years	Four regional Colleges of Education
Training of higher education teachers	Colleges of education	Not mentioned	M. Ed. and PhD Degree	2 and 3 years	University
Technical and vocational school teachers	All levels	Instructor Training Certificate I.T.C.	Dipl. in Engineering etc.	1 year	Central Training Institutes

Instructors in technical and vocational schools are normally trained in Central Training Institutes (CTIs), which offer one-year courses providing training in skills development and principles of teaching. Graduates of these institutions are awarded an Instructor Training Certificate.

The National Council for Teacher Education is entrusted by The Central Government with all matters concerning teacher education of India, including. quality, content and evaluation.

Competence levels obtained at institutions providing teacher education and training.

NATIONAL COUNCIL OF TEACHER EDUCATION (NCTE)

During our meeting with NCTE, we got the impression of a competent organ deeply involved in development of teacher education. NCTE is committed to, among other things, developing the quality of teacher education

The role of NCTE is to unify and regularise teacher training. An Act of Parliament in 1993 gave it statutory powers regarding recognition of teacher education institutions, staffing and teacher education programmes as well as the means to develop teacher education.

About 2000 teacher education institutions are engaged in the preparation of teachers for different school stages.

Teacher training as an integral part of the Indian education system started with the first normal schools in India in 1856. The Indian Education Commission approved introduction of separate teacher education programmes for elementary and secondary teachers in 1882.

Today, according to NCTE, teacher education for primary education is comparable to international standards in many states. However, the same cannot be said about the preparation of secondary, vocational and pre-school teachers.

So internship, practice of teaching, practical activities and supplementary educational activities as part of teacher education still need to be developed, concludes NCTE.

Unit V

India is mainly an importer of higher education. To a smaller degree, the country is also an exporter of educational programmes. In response to globalisation, the UGC has initiated a programme for the Promotion of Indian Higher Education Abroad (PIHEAD), which will run through the tenth five-year plan (2002-07).

Education in India is considered to be a social service and is accorded the status of public good. The recognition of the education sector as a tradable service sector under the General Agreement on Trade and Services (GATS) – World Trade Organisation (WTO) regime has challenged India's understanding of education as a social service.

In the absence of any national policy to regulate the foreign education service providers, India has witnessed liberalisation of the sector. Thus, the presence of foreign universities in India may, in future, turn towards commercialisation against Central government's or the Supreme Court's view that education is not for profit.

According to WES, the UGC expresses concern about the commercial presence of foreign educational institutions and fears that higher education will be limited to the select few as there will be a high price for acquiring any foreign degree. Another concern is that commercialisation will promote privatization that will, in turn, increase the cost of higher education.

There is concern among the public that commercialisation will adversely affect public higher education and fear that the government may slowly withdraw from its commitments to higher education, seeing that the alternate mechanism of funding is gaining support from international sources. They also fear that

Quality assurance of transnational education is not specifically conducted by any accrediting councils, due to the fact that India has no national regulation on this type of education.

However, the UGC under the Ministry of Human Resources and Development, Distance Education Council, and AICTE are involved in this field. Transnational education offered by Indian higher education institutions has to be recognised by the UGC; see "Guidelines and Practices in the Field of Trans-National Educations" in http://www.ugc.ac.in .

In 2005, AICTE has drawn up a fresh set of regulations to monitor foreign technical education institutions and prevent the entry of non-accredited institutes into the country. The new rules will replace the earlier mandate issued by the AICTE in April 2003.

Under the new system, foreign institutions will be treated on a par with Indian technical institutions and will be governed by AICTE guidelines. They will not be allowed to appoint additional campuses in India. "Education innovations, including experimentation with different modes of delivery by a foreign university, shall be allowed, provided such a system is well established either in their parent country or in India," state the regulations on the AICTE website. AICTE will stipulate the fee and the intake for each course to be offered by foreign education providers.

5.1 FOREIGN INSTITUTIONS IN INDIA

The 1990s saw the emergence of foreign universities operating in India in collaboration with private institutions in the country. A research study conducted by *National Institute of Educational Planning and Administration* (NIEPA) in 2005 on 'Foreign Education Providers in India' brings out some of the salient features of their operation. There were 131 Indian institutions collaborating with foreign institutions. The list, however, may not be fully exhaustive.

It may be observed that in some states the foreign education providers were concentrated in metropolitan cities and some other cities where the prospects of vocational courses exist on a large scale. Information also shows that, at present, only the USA and the UK have shown interest in collaborating with Indian partners. There are other potential countries such as Australia, New Zealand and Canada who are watching the developments and the government stand on any regulation regarding Foreign Education Providers. At present these countries are organising educational fairs and have also representatives to attract Indian students to their respective countries.

The majority of the foreign education providers provide professional/vocational courses. Of the total sample of 131 institutions (2005), 107 were providing vocational courses, 19 technical courses and only 5 were offering general education. The data show that, in the category of vocational courses, management courses are the most popular. Business Management and Hotel Management constitute approximately 80% of the total number of courses.

The commercial presence of foreign institutions has led to multiple methods of collaboration for delivering foreign programmes. The collaborative arrangement under the commercial presence varies from institution to institution. There are, in general, three existing and one possible categories of delivery of foreign programmes in India.

TYPES OF OPERATION OF FOREIGN INSTITUTIONS IN INDIA

Types of Collaboration	Numbers of collaboration
Twinning Arrangement	30
Franchise	2
Offshore Campus/Branch Campus	0
Programmatic collaboration include joint course design, credit transfer etc.	18

Source: Above result is based on a sample of 50 institutions, taken from 'Foreign Education Providersin India', NIEPA, New Delhi, 2005.

The table shows that most programmes are offered under the twinning arrangement. In fact, this is one of the preferred methods for the foreign institution to attract international students to the home country. Under twinning, the movement of students from one country to another enables them to obtain the foreign degree at a relatively lower cost since part of the course is undertaken in the host country.

The programmatic collaboration that consists of joint courses and joint degree provision by the institutions of the home and the host countries ranks second in India in terms of the supply of education services by foreign institutions. The reason is that the Indian partner may prefer to design a programme with the inputs received from the foreign institution and offer the whole programme in India to make it cost competitive. Another reason may be that, through this mode, Indian private partners prefer to have a brand name of a foreign university in the absence of any regulation allowing private institutions to award the degree.

Franchising is one of the modes of operation, which is a kind of collaboration between a foreign institution and an Indian university where the exporting and awarding institution controls course design and delegates course delivery to the importing Indian university.

There are only two such institutions in India. The fourth category in which the foreign education providers can show their presence is that of branch campuses. None of the foreign institutions presently come under this category, perhaps because there is no domestic regulation for the operation of foreign institutions in India. The absence of such concrete regulation inhibits growth, due to the investment in infrastructure required to open branch campuses. Once such regulation is in place, the number of branch campuses might increase.

INDIAN INSTITUTIONS ABROAD

Many Indian institutions have opened branch campuses abroad. However, the number of such institutions abroad is smaller than that of foreign institutions in India. In the higher education segment, they include some deemed-to-be universities such as Birla Institute of Technology Pillani, Manipal Academy for Higher Education (MAHE), and private institutions such as NIIT India (this last is a private institution which is applying for recognition as a deemed-to be university; see List of Proposals for the Grant of Deemed University

Received and Screened up to 17 February, 2005 at http://www.ugc.ac.in/inside/receivedproposal.pdf).

Additionally, some public institutions like Delhi University, Indira Gandhi National Open University (IGNOU), Shreemati Nathibhai Damodar Thackersey (SNDT) College, Mysore University and Madras University are making their presence felt abroad. The Government of India has taken various initiatives to promote Indian education abroad. In April 2002, it established the Committee on Promotion of Indian Education Abroad (COPIEA) under the chairmanship of the Secretary, Department of Secondary & Higher Education. The COPIEA will monitor all activities aimed at promoting Indian education abroad and will regulate the operation of foreign educational institutions to safeguard the interests of students and the larger national interest as well.

To this end, a system of registration will be introduced under which institutions will have to furnish information on operations and adhere to certain guidelines relating to publicity, maintenance of standards, charging of fees, granting of degrees etc. The COPIEA will, over a period of time, develop a sectoral policy on foreign direct investment in the education sector. (10th Five-year plan).

REGIONAL CONVENTION

There is a regional convention of UNESCO which is called "Regional Convention on the Recognition of Studies, Diplomas and Degrees in Higher Education in Asia and the Pacific", which was signed by 33 countries (including India) in the region in 1983. India ratified the convention in 2000.

This convention is similar to the Lisbon Convention in Europe. It paves the way for academic mobility among the Asian countries. The contracting states intend to promote collaboration in education and research. In order to achieve this goal, the convention defines the areas and methods of recognition of foreign certificates, diplomas or degrees of higher education in the region.

Unit VI

QUALITY ASSURANCE

6.1 GENERAL EDUCATION

There is no overall quality assurance body within secondary and higher secondary education with the power to monitor the quality of secondary educational institutions and establish sanctions if the standard of quality is not adhered to.

The National Council of Education Research and Training (NCERT) is empowered to elaborate the national curriculum framework as part of the concurrent subjects in the India constitution. The authority of implementation of curricula and quality assurance lies with the provinces and the boards of secondary education.

As NCERT has noted, standards vary from state to state as well as from board to board. The Central Board of Second Education (CBSE) and the Council for Indian School Certificate Examinations (CISCE) are generally recognised as competent bodies regarding quality assurance, and so are some state boards. CBSE, for example, has worked out detailed rules for affiliation and examination and also has procedures for regular revision of the curriculum.

Reports (see literature list) note particularly the lack of trained teachers within rural primary education as well as the high teacher absenteeism rate as an impediment to quality in teaching.

6.2 TEACHER EDUCATION

The National Council of Teacher Education (NCTE) as a statutory body came into existence in pursuance of the National Council for Teacher Education Act, 1993 (No.73 of 1993) in 1995. The mandate given to NCTE includes research and training of persons for equipping them to teach at pre-primary, primary, secondary and senior secondary stages in schools, and non-formal education institutions, part-time education, adult education and distance (correspondence) education courses. NCTE has headquarters in New Delhi and four Regional Committees spread across the country. NCTE performs both institution and programme accreditation. Its accreditation process is laid down in the above-mentioned act enacted by the Indian Parliament. The process can be summed up as follows:

- Application for recognition submitted to the Regional Committee
- Regional Committee decides whether the institution has adequate financial resources, accommodation, library, qualified staff, laboratory, fulfils conditions required for proper functioning for a course or training in teacher education
- Recognition
- Results published in an Official Gazette
- Non-recognition will lead to discontinuing of the course or training in teacher education

If a teacher education institution is accredited by NCTE, it is automatically granted affiliation to a university. NCTE can also withdraw accreditation from an institution. The withdrawal is also published in an Official Gazette for general information. In this case, the institution automatically loses its affiliation. A list of accredited

programmes and institutions by NCTE is provided in
http://www.nctein.org with detailed information on the duration and
level of teaching qualifications (preprimary, primary, secondary, senior
secondary, etc.).

6.3 TECHNICAL AND VOCATIONAL EDUCATION

The Vocational Training/Craftsmen Courses are offered at the
Industrial Training Institutes. The Diploma courses are offered in the
Polytechnics which are widely spread throughout the states and Union
Territories. These polytechnics are affiliated to the respective State
Boards of Technical Education which lay down in general the levels and
standards of the courses and guide the system of evaluation of the
students sitting examinations. Degree and Post-Graduate courses are
offered in colleges affiliated to the various Universities, certain
University Departments, and institutions declared to be of national
importance or deemed to be universities.

The All India Council of Technical Education (AICTE) is responsible
for quality assurance of technical and vocational education in India. In
order to assess the qualitative competence of educational programmes in
engineering and related areas from the diploma level to the postgraduate
level, the National Board of Accreditation (NBA) was established in
1994 under section 10(u) of AICTE Act, 1987. While the AICTE takes
care of the regulatory role, the NBA performs programme accreditation.
The NBA makes recommendations to the AICTE for recognition or
derecognition of institutions or programmes, while the AICTE approves
new institutions and new programmes. There has been an accelerated

effort to accredit programmes. The total number of programmes accredited is 1,522. (See the figure below)

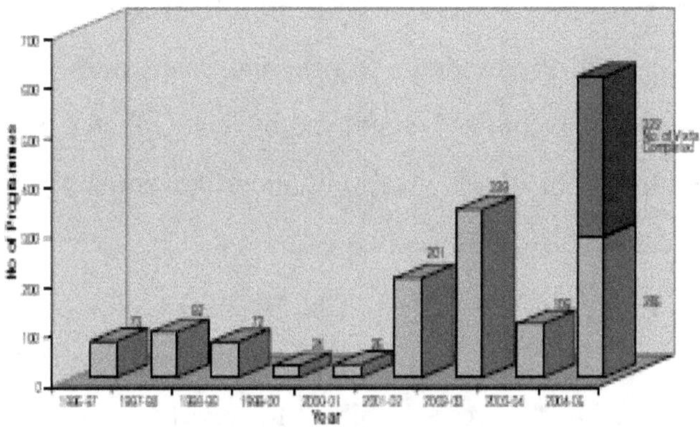

The NBA's accreditation procedure comprises the following steps: The institution submits an application with information/data provided by the NBA. An accreditation team constituted by the NBA visits the institution and make its recommendations. Accreditation is awarded by the NBA. The result is notified and published in the Directory of Accredited Programmes of Institutions.

The NBA has prescribed accreditation criteria for undergraduate and post-graduate programmes. The criteria for undergraduate programmes are: organization and governance, human resource facility-faculty & staff, students, finance & physical resources, mission, goals, research & development, industry-institution interaction, research and development, supplementary process, teaching-learning process. NBA's accreditation is periodical and valid for 3-5 years.

6.4 HIGHER EDUCATION

India has had a well-developed quality assurance (QA) system since independence in 1947. The QA system is embodied in regulations covering nearly all the fields of studies and professions. In India, the establishment of universities is regulated by law. Only the parliament of the Government of India (central/union government) and state legislation can establish a university.

Various apex institutions have been entrusted, either by an Act of Parliament or by an Act of Legislative Assembly or by central or state governments, with the responsibility to regulate the standards of education. For example, the University Grants Commission (UGC) was established by the UGC Act, 1956, to coordinate and maintain standards of university education. The NAAC was established in 1994 under 12cc of the UGC Act to assess the standards of quality. It assesses and accredits universities along with their constituent and affiliated colleges.

Similarly, as mentioned earlier, the AICTE was established under the AICTE Act 1987 to plan and coordinate the development of technical education system in the country. Under Section 10 (U) of the AICTE Act, the National Board of Accreditation (NBA) has been set up to assess and accredit the technical institutions in the country and to make recommendations to the relevant authorities for recognition and derecognition of qualifications.

Furthermore, the National Council of Teacher Education (NCTE) was established in 1995. A list of statutory bodies which regulate the standards of education in various professional fields is provided in the appendix 1.

6.5 NAAC Initiative

To ensure quality in higher education institutions, the National Assessment and Accreditation Council (NAAC) was established on 16 September 1994 as an autonomous affiliate of the UGC.

The NAAC is different from the other accreditation agencies which accredit programmes and institutions in the field of professional studies, in that it is an autonomous body and can accredit all kinds of higher education institutions, both general, teacher, technical and professional, and in that it is not mandatory to be regulated by the NAAC, even though a few states have made it so. The professional accrediting agencies conduct assessment and accreditation of programmes or institutes within their respective domains.

Many specialized institutes that the professional accreditation agencies have accredited have also volunteered for institutional accreditation by the NAAC. Quite a few engineering, medical, fine arts, law and management institutes, for example, have been accredited by the NAAC.

The delegation encountered different attitudes towards external quality assurance. Some of the universities, particularly the young ones, argued in favour of the external quality assurance, as a means to guarantee standards and attract students. Others were opposed to external quality assurance. Institutions gave several reasons for resistance to accreditation, including a lack of resources, documentation and/or time to carry out self-assessment. In addition, administrators at affiliated colleges feel that autonomous institutions have an unfair advantage because autonomy allows for greater flexibility in programme structure, use of funds and teaching strategies.

Perhaps the most compelling argument for rejection of the NAAC is the fact that so few of the most reputable institutions in India have initiated the assessment process; they simply do not rely on an external agency's endorsement. The reputable India Institute of Science has preferred not to be accredited by NAAC. When asked for the reason for this, the answer from the Director of International Relations of the Institute was that they did not need any accreditation to assure quality of education.

The *NAAC* applies the following criteria in assessment and accreditation: curricular aspects, teaching, learning and evaluation, research, consultancy and extension, infrastructure and learning resources, student support and progression, organisation and management and healthy practices.

The accreditation process that the NAAC applies follows these 5 steps:

- Developing the National framework for degrees and programmes;
- An institution prepares and submits a self-study report.

- A peer team visits the HE institution and writes a report and make recommendations to the NAAC.

- The NAAC certifies the final accreditation.

- The NAAC publicly announces the accreditation outcome. An institution can make an appeal against the outcome. The NAAC conducts two types of accreditation, i.e. institution and programme assessment. Accreditation by the NAAC is valid for 5 years.

Due to the high number of higher education institutions in the country, the NAAC currently gives priority to assessment of institutions which are funded by the UGC. The NAAC has so far accredited 2,088 colleges and 113 universities in India (2005). The analysis of accreditation of 55 universities show that 16 universities obtained B++, 24 universities obtained lower than B++ and only 15 universities obtained higher than a B++ grade. Of 1,717 colleges accredited, 425 received B+ and 845 colleges received lower than a B+ grade, whereas 447 colleges received better than a B+ grade.

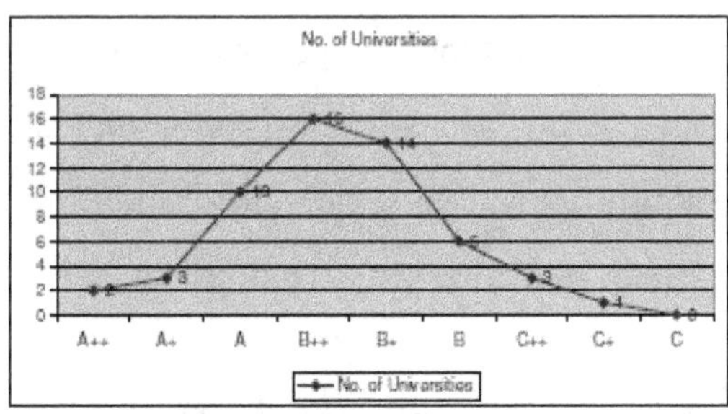

As shown in the figure above, A++ is the highest grade, with C as the lowest; the scale on the left is the number of universities, from 0 to 18.

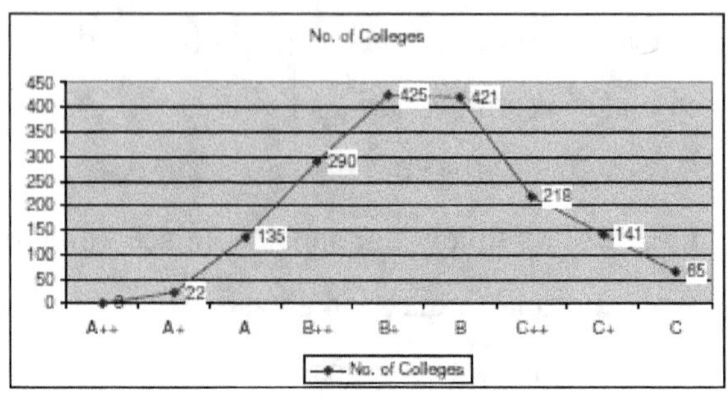

Since there are many other national councils also responsible for quality assurance in higher education in professional fields of study, the NAAC is trying now to link all quality assurance agencies in accreditation work. For example, it cooperates with the National Council of Teacher Education (NCTE) on the accreditation of teacher training institutions.

6.6 QUALITY ASSURANCE AT STATE LEVEL

In a country of India's size, there are bound to be differences in quality. The NAAC has been able to identify high quality colleges and universities through the process of external accreditation. It is necessary to develop a quality drive, through individual institutions' own internal quality assurance systems and through government initiatives to upgrade quality, since quality is the prime concern in the mutual recognition of degrees. As a starting point, the quality institutions identified by the NAAC can play a part in the process of mutual recognition of degrees in India.

One of the intentions of establishing the NAAC was to tackle the quality problem in Indian higher education institutions, where the states, rather than the central government, exercise major responsibility for higher education. Thus, the NAAC functions as a national quality maintenance actor across the higher education sector. This strength of the NAAC can be demonstrated, for instance, by the cooperation between the Department of Collegiate Education of the Government of Karnataka State and the NAAC.

The state has made the accreditation of a higher education institution by the NAAC a prerequisite for grants from the state government and has signed a Memorandum of Understanding with the NAAC. The purpose of the memorandum is to provide a policy framework, direction, coordination and leadership for disseminating "Total Quality Management" in all the institutions leading up to NAAC accreditation in the state in the long term. By so doing, the state has implemented quality assurance work at state level. The state has mandated all the higher education institutions within the territory to establish in-house quality assurance departments. In this state alone, there are 86 government colleges and 277 private aided colleges which have been accredited by the NAAC, 1 government college and 5 aided colleges which have been given autonomy, 22 government colleges which have been identified for NAAC assessment.

Unit VII

Indian Education System – Issues and Challenges

7.1 Need and Importance of Education

Education, as you are aware, is vital to the human resources development and empowerment in the stages of growth of a nation. In any education system, higher education encompassing Management, Engineering, Medicines etc., plays a major role in imparting knowledge, values, and developing skills and, in the process, increase the growth and productivity of the nation. While the Government is committed to providing primary education and certain facilities/subsidies for higher education, given the higher cost involved in the establishment of higher education institutes, we are witnessing the entry of private sector to run educational institutions.

On the need for education, I wish to quote our Father of the Nation, Mahatma Gandhi, who once said that education not only moulds the new generation, but reflects a society's fundamental assumptions about itself and the individuals which compose it. The famous philosopher Einstein while discussing the need for education has projected the following fundamentals:

- To educate the individual as a free individual; to understand and use critical thinking skills.

- To educate the individual as a part of society – virtually all our knowledge, our clothes, our food is produced by others in our society, thus, we owe Society and have responsibility to contribute back to Society.

- Through education, knowledge must continually be renewed by ceaseless effort, if it is not to be lost. It resembles a statute of marble which stands in the desert and is continually threatened with burial by the shifting sand. The hands of service must ever be at work, in order that the marble continue to lastingly shine in the sun.

While discussing the importance of education, I must state that schools have become the most important means of transforming wealth of knowledge and skills from one generation to another. However, the role of institutions becomes more challenging in the modern world institutions should be viewed as an investment for economic prosperity.

In India, there are about 26,478 institutions providing higher education and accounting for the largest number in the world. In comparison, according to a report1, in 2010, the U.S. had only 6,706 higher education schools and China had 4,000. It is important that given the large number of schools of higher learning in India, we must target to bring more students under the system. Investment in human capital, lifelong learning and quality education help in the development of society and nation.

DEMOGRAPHIC CONTOUR

According to the National Commission on Population, it is expected that the age profile of population of India will experience changes in the coming years. By 2016, approximately 50 per cent of the total population will be in the age group of 15–25 years. It is projected that a vast population would enter the working age group in the next 15 years, leading to increase in productive activities and also savings rate as witnessed in Japan in the 1950s and China 1980s. In other words, there would be a tremendous rise in the number of employable work force in the job market which would demand commensurate investment in education. In the literature, Demographic Dividend refers to population "lump" in the working age group of 15–60 which can be described as a major advantage for pushing the economic growth. It suggests that the major challenge before India is how this advantageous demographic profile can be harnessed to reflect in the macro-economic parameters of the country.Given the demographic profile advantage, the average Indian will be only 29 years old in 2020 as compared with 37 years for China and the U.S., 45 years for West Europe and 48 years for Japan.2 The global demographic profile, in future, would, therefore, lead to shortage of productive workforce globally but India will experience a surplus. We need to realize that this advantage for us will not be automatically transformed into higher economic growth. Strategic interventions and foresight in terms of encouraging investments in education and skills development by policy makers are needed to reap maximum benefits of demographic dividend.

7.2 ISSUES AND CHALLENGES

EXPENDITURE ON EDUCATION

In terms of expenditure incurred on education, particularly on higher education, during the year 2010–11, the government spent around Rs.15, 440 crore which is about 85 per cent of the revised budget estimates for the year. The recent 66th round of NSSO survey reveals that between 1999 and 2009, spending on education in general jumped by 378 per cent in rural areas and 345 per cent in urban areas of the country. The survey further reveals that spending on children's education underlines sharp increase – 63 per cent for rural and 73 per cent for urban families. However, if we measure the expenses on education as a percentage to GDP, India lags behind some developed/ developing nations (Table 1). We recognize that the gap in investments in education in India can perhaps be filled by private sector playing a crucial role.

GROSS ENROLMENT PATTERN

At present, in India, there are about 1.86 crore students enrolled in various streams of higher education including Business Management.3 Despite the large number of students studying in various streams, we have not seen any major shift in the productivity as skills and talents are deficient to support economic activities and, hence, there is a serious concern on employability of these educated persons. The gross enrolment ratio (GER) for higher education in India was 12 per cent in 2010. However, the enrolment level varies across states. We also need to recognize that our enrolment level is far below several other countries. For example, according to a Report, GER is 23 per cent for China, 34 per cent for Brazil, 57 per cent for U.K., 77 per cent for both Australia and Russia and 83 per cent for the U.S (Appendix 4). In this context, the attempt of Government authorities to increase the number of students by 2020 so as to reach GER of 30 per cent becomes a big challenge. No doubt, the launch of new institutes like JRE School of Management can play a catalyst role in addressing the challenge of increasing GER in India. As a positive step, for the remaining duration of Eleventh Five Year Plan, the Government has taken initiatives to incentivise States for setting up/expansion of existing educational institutions, establishment of 8 universities, expansion of colleges to achieve a target of 1 lakh students enrolment and schemes for setting up model colleges in regions which are below national average of GER.

Table 1: Expenditure on Education

Country	Spending on education as a % of GDP	Country	Spending on education as a % of GDP
Switzerland	5.8	South Africa	5.3
U.S.	5.7	Thailand	5.2
France	5.6	Chile	4.2
U.K.	5.3	Brazil	4.2
Malaysia	8.1	India	4.1
Mexico	5.3	Russia	3.8

Note: Government education expenditure as a percentage of GDP (2000–2002).

Source: United Nations Human Development Programme.

CAPACITY UTILIZATION

Another challenge to be addressed in strengthening the Indian education system is to improve the capacity utilization. For example, a recent study4 on capacity utilization in India for higher education indicates that the capacity utilization in case of MBA is about 57 per cent in Maharashtra and 72 per cent in Haryana (Appendix 5). In case of certain states, there are a lot of unfilled seats in institutions. On the one hand, we need to improve our GER, and on the other, we need to ensure that institutions/ colleges/schools created for providing higher education fully utilize the capacity created.

INFRASTRUCTURE FACILITIES

One of the factors why the capacity utilization is low in upcoming/new institutions/colleges (both in private and public sectors) is their inability to provide necessary physical infrastructure to run the institutions. The infrastructure facilities desirable to rank the institutions of better quality include real estate, state of the art class rooms, library, hostels, furniture, sports facilities, transport, commercial buildings, etc. We need to ensure apolitical private sector participation in the establishment of colleges for providing quality physical infrastructure.

PPP MODEL

The Government is making efforts to improve the education system in terms of various parameters like GER, quality, investments, infrastructure, etc. But we need to recognize the constraints for the Government to make a big turnaround with huge investments in education. I believe that private sector has started playing a distinctive role in improving the education system in India. In this context, it is useful to explore the possibility of public private partnership (PPP) model in education. This is not only going to reduce the burden of the Government in incurring high cost of providing basic infrastructure facilities but also lead to construction of state of the art buildings, labs, libraries, hostels etc. Besides, the collaborative efforts between universities/colleges and corporates would help in organizing joint research and development, students getting exposure to industrial activities in terms of internships, corporate training during vacations and issuing of certificates by corporates for attending internship/training etc. and, thus, facilitating in image building and branding of institutions and making the students more job-worthy.

STUDENT-TEACHER RATIO

Another challenge for improving the Indian education system is to improve the student teacher ratio. In India, this ratio is very high as compared to certain comparable countries in the world. For example, while in developed countries this ratio stands at 11.4, in case of India, it is as high as 22.0. It is even low in CIS (10.9), Western Asia (15.3), and Latin America (16.6) (Appendix 6). This brings the necessity to recruit quality teachers and strengthen the teachers required to handle classes. I also feel that like in developed countries where students are given part-time teaching assignments, we can also explore such possibilities in technical/higher education to handle lower level classes. It is also expected to help the students in meeting their education expenses partially.

ACCREDITATION AND BRANDING – QUALITY STANDARDS

In order to improve the skills and talent of our large populace, there is a need for raising the quality and standards of our education system. It is well-known that many of our professionals (engineers/doctors/management professionals) remain unemployed despite lot of opportunities being open in the globalised world. One of the major factors is the lack of quality education resulting in qualified but not employable category. We need to introduce/activate the mechanism for rating and ranking universities/colleges. At present, there is no compulsion for institutions/colleges to get accreditation in India. Government has already mooted a proposal to introduce accreditation. We, therefore, require standard rating agencies to give accreditation to universities/colleges/schools. In a recent ranking of Business Schools by Financial Times at global level, in the top fifteen, only two of the Indian premier Business Schools appeared at rank no. 11 and 13 for the year 2011. Most of the top ranking business schools were from the U.S. In this ranking, even China was ahead of India. In the same reporting, in respect of value for money of these two Schools, it is observed that it is not that high when compared with some of the best U.S. Schools. However, a positive development is that these high ranked Indian Schools possess faculties with doctoral qualifications and of global standards who can deliver quality education to the students. In the world ranking of universities by Quacquarelli Symonds in 2010, out of 200 world renowned universities, only one Indian educational institution appears in the list, while 53 institutions are in the U.S. According to Webometrics ranking for 2011, while no Indian university appears in the list, there are 99 U.S. universities included. This essentially shows that we need to develop Centre for excellence of global standards. Given the increasing role of private sector in the recent years in the development of higher education standards, we need more such institutions that meet certain global rating standards to come up in those areas where low GER prevails. I understand that the JRE School of Management has been established in collaboration with the largest private education group in Asia-Pacific and, hence, striving for quality education of global standards would be its principal aim.

STUDENTS STUDYING ABROAD

As mentioned in the beginning of my address, India has the largest number of higher education institutions. Despite that, we find the number of students interested in pursuing higher studies abroad is on the rise. In the year 2006, according to a Wikipedia report, 1.23 lakh students opted for higher education abroad, of which about 76,000 chose the U.S. as their destination, followed by U.K., Canada and Australia. However, in 2010–11, about 1.03 lakh students got admission to study in the U.S. In regard to Australia also, the number is on the rise. During 2004 to 2009, the number of students joining different courses rose from 30,000 to 97,000. Likewise, in the other sought after destination of U.K. for higher education, students studying abroad doubled between 1999 and 2009. In 2009, about 19,205 students were studying in U.K. Various factors encourage Indian students to seek admission abroad by taking loans from financial institutions including (a) quality of education, (b) increasing prosperity and aspirations and (c) social prestige and also exposure and experiences gained. We have to recognize these short-comings while building our educational institutions for reversal of trend.

7.3 ROLE OF RBI AND COMMERCIAL BANKS

Now, I would like to dwell upon the role played by Reserve Bank of India (RBI) and the banking system in India in strengthening education system. Realizing the importance of education for the economic development and the overall living standards, the RBI is involved in formulating progressive and proactive policy guidelines for lending to education by the banking system.

- The RBI, in view of the importance of education and the need to bring more students under the category of "education loans", has classified such loans and advances granted to individuals for educational purposes up to Rs. 10 lakh for studies in India and Rs. 20 lakh for studies abroad, under "priority sector".

- In June 2004, the scope of definition of "infrastructure lending" was expanded to include construction of educational institutions. Accordingly, schools and colleges can now avail bank finance for improving their infrastructure. The available figures (covering about 63 per cent of banks under the category of "infrastructure"), indicate the share of outstanding loans to educational institutions in the total infrastructure lending of commercial banks was 1.5 per cent for end-March 2011.

- RBI has been liberalizing foreign exchange rules for acquiring education from institutions abroad. A student can draw foreign exchange equivalent to USD 10,000 under private visit quota at the time of going abroad. The limit of USD 30,000 for education abroad on declaration basis was enhanced to USD 1,00,000 since July 17, 2003. In addition, a student can also draw foreign exchange equivalent to USD 2,00,000 for education purposes under liberalized remittance scheme before leaving the country i.e. before he/she gains the status of non-resident. Students can avail loan from a bank abroad for study purposes on the basis of counter guarantee given by an Indian Bank under approval route.

- With a view to facilitate banks, the Indian Banks' Association has brought out a model scheme for educational loan in the year 2001 which was again revised in January 2010 and got circulated to all member banks for implementation. This would facilitate economically weaker sections of the society to avail educational loans from scheduled banks with modified easier norms. In recent years, there has been a remarkable spurt in the disbursal of educational loans by commercial banks. The educational loans outstanding amounted to Rs.27,709 crore as at end March 2009 which increased to up to Rs.42,808 crore as at end-March 2011 Table 2).

Table 2: Educational Loan of Scheduled Commercial Banks

Particulars	Mar-09	Mar-10	Mar-11
Amount outstanding (In Rs Crore)	27709.5	36359.7	42808.1
No of accounts (In Lakh)	16.3	19.7	22.8

We have nominated a nodal officer at the Central office of the RBI for the purpose of all educational loan issues/grievances.

- Apart from policy formulation, as an institution also, RBI undertakes activities to educate students relating to central banking, banking and financial system. Illustratively, to educate young scholars, a scheme has been introduced in which every year RBI selects a good number of scholars from different region of the country. In addition, RBI has set up research and training institution for banking technology.

7.4 WAY FORWARD

INNOVATIONS REQUIRED

The challenge of educating millions of young people implies that we need to scale up our educational efforts multi-fold despite having the largest number of higher education institutes in the world. Mr Shantanu Prakash has established one more institute today but we need to create many more such centres. Scaling up is not possible unless the students become successful, create value in the society and contribute back to their alma-mater or, better still, start new institutes of global standards themselves.

The curriculum of some of the colleges/universities is more or less obsolete and do not equip students with the necessary skills or impart latest knowledge. If a student passes out of a chosen course, he or she should be employable as a work force. Unfortunately, given the phenomenal share of lack of technical knowledge in the courses of education, students are found wanting in the desired skills and technical soundness. To address this issue, we may think of strengthening the vocational streams in schools/colleges. I urge the universities/schools/colleges to regularly revisit their curriculum by involving experts from different fields so that the curriculum can lead to knowledge development. Further, why can we not use the available infrastructure more intensely? For instance, why cannot a second stream of courses, say vocational, be run in the evening/night so that the available /created infrastructure is better utilized.

Teachers are the most important factors for any innovative society because teachers' knowledge and skills not only enhance quality and efficacy of education, but also improve the potential for research and innovation. Given the higher level of GER to be achieved by 2020, a large number of teachers would be required to educate the growing young population.

Maybe, students could be used as teachers, especially good students coming from lower income groups so that they can be partly be compensated. Further, barring some leading schools/universities/autonomous educational institutions, many of the teachers of colleges/universities need to hone their skills/talent. There is a need to encourage teachers to participate by presenting research papers in seminars/workshops/conferences and receive periodic trainings for updation of knowledge/skills. It is equally important that a feedback mechanism from students is introduced in universities/colleges to assess and evaluate teachers' role in the institutional developmental process.

QUALITY OF EDUCATION

Given that we need to compete globally in the 21st century, our education system should adopt certain benchmarking techniques for improving instruction models and administrative procedures in universities/colleges to move forward. I suggest that we need a thorough study and evaluation of models implemented elsewhere and work out strategies to adopt such models in our system. Benchmarking in my opinion would provide benefits to our education system in terms of reengineering, setting right objectives, etc.

The country is showing consistency in economic growth pattern, leading the world in terms of information and technology, modernization various economic activities and pushing for higher share of industries and services sectors of the economy but there is one area which needs reform is "education system". While it is true that some investments are taking place in the country's higher education system, we are yet to establish world class research facilities, recruiting profound academicians in universities/colleges/research institutions, etc. to sustain and forge lead in economic development. It is important to understand that countries like China, Singapore, South Korea, etc. are moving fast in investing in education system. Therefore, it is imperative that our educational institutions are equipped with the desired quality and standards which are essentials for transforming the younger workforce into productive ones. Needless to reiterate that in the higher education system focus on use of technology for effective learning by students also need to be encouraged to have cutting edge over our competitors in the globalised world.

MAKING EDUCATION AFFORDABLE

In India, if education has to reach all deserving students, it should be made affordable. The fee structure in Government owned/sponsored institutions is inexpensive in India. However, in some private sector institutions, which have the freedom to prescribe fee structure and despite broad guidelines from certain state governments, fees are beyond the capacity of poor and deserving students. Ideally, the fee structure should vary for such economically weaker students. I would urge the educators to keep in mind that education should not become prohibitively expensive and ensure that no deserving candidate is denied admission just for the fact that he or she does not possess the necessary financial resources.

ETHICS IN EDUCATION

In my opinion, the most important objective of any educational institution is to equip the students with ethical values besides imparting knowledge and skills. Today, I find that this basic human quality is slowly eroding. Illustratively, while the RBI as well as Government of India is formulating progressive policies to ensure funds do not pose a major problem for education, I observe some disturbing trend in respect of repayment of loans by students. It may be noted if the loans are not repaid after it falls due, the non-performing assets of banks will increase and in the process, banks are likely to be skeptical in sanctioning educational loans. It is, therefore, important that the repayment schedules are adhered to by those students who have taken loans. It is understood that to encourage banks to give educational loans to all deserving students, the Government is looking into the issue of setting up of a system of insuring educational loans. To reduce default of education loans, I strongly feel that the School Alumni Association of students can become active in inculcating ethics and values among students. They can provide the required synergies and linkages in addressing challenges relating to non-payment of outstanding education loans.

In the same coin, as education has to be made affordable to all deserving and poor students, there is a strong need for educational institutions not to over-commercialize education but to uphold ethics in the business of education as well. It is not anyone's case that the business has to be run unprofitably but the business must be carried out with ethical values for sustenance of educational institutions. Over exploitation should be avoided. Profit cannot be the sole motive for undertaking this business. It must be driven by an unflinching commitment to society which in turn will benefit the business in the long run.

To sum up, we need to recognize that the knowledge, skills and productivity of our growing young and dynamic work force forms the backbone of our economy. To reap the benefits of such a young work force, we need to implement the reforms in the education system and also bring forth new factors of production, namely knowledge, skills and technology which have the ability to unleash the productive frontiers of the economy in the most efficient and dynamic way. Besides, taking a leaf from the western hemisphere, India should try to become "knowledge economy" to promote inclusive growth. I, therefore, would like underline three major areas to be focused to ensure that our education system is sustainable and meets global standards:

- Quality of Education – in terms of infrastructure, teachers, accreditation, etc.
- Affordability of Education – ensuring poor and deserving students are not denied education.
- Ethics in Education – avoiding over-commercialization of education system.

7.5 THE ROLE OF GOVERNMENT OF INDIA IN EDUCATION

One of the major educational controversies today refers to the role of the Government of India in education. Prima facie education is a State subject. Entry 11 of the List II of the Seventh Schedule to the Constitution lays down that "education including universities, subject to the provisions of Entries 63, 64, 65 and 66 of List I and Entry 25 of List III" should be a State subject. But there are some other provisions in the Constitution itself which contradict the almost absolute delegation of authority suggested by this entry in the State list; and what is even more significant, the Central Government has since shown an unprecedented activity and interest in the field of education ever since the attainment of independence. In 1947, it appointed a University Commission and has since been engaged in evolving common policies in Higher education such as the introduction of the three-year degree course. This was followed by a Secondary Education Commission which tried to introduce a number of uniform trends in a field where the Centre has had hardly any constitutional authority. No Commission was appointed in the field of Primary education. But the scheme of Basic education was declared to have gone beyond the stage of experimentation and was also adopted as the national pattern at the Elementary stage. The interest of the Central Government in Technical education and scientific research has been too obvious to need any illustration. Besides, an innumerable number of Committees and Reports have tried to iron out an all-India thought, policy and programme in almost every sector of education. Of still greater importance is the revival of the Central grants for education which had been discontinued in 1918-1919. In the period of post-war reconstruction as well as in the first and second Plans, substantial grants were given to the States towards the implementation of a large variety of educational programmes. With the adoption of the technique of Five Year Plans and the creation of the Planning Commission, the real authority to determine policies, priorities and programmes has now passed on from the States to the Centre in most sectors of development; and as a corollary to this major shift in all developmental activity, it is alleged that the, educational progress in the States is now more dependent upon the financial allocations and priorities decided at the Centre by the Planning Commission and the Ministry of Education than upon any decision taken by the States at their own level. In short, the trend to centralisation in policy-making in all fields of education has been the most dominating note of this period and it has had hardly any parallel in our educational history except for the brief spell under Lord Curzon.

The reactions at the Centre and in the States to these developments have been extremely divergent. On the one hand, the State Governments have grown more and more critical and resentful of this policy. They claim that Education is essentially their preserve; that they understand their educational needs much better than the Centre itself; and that the attempt of the Centre to cut into their sphere has generally done more harm than good to the cause of education. They also plead that Central grants should be placed at the disposal of the States without any strings attached and they are extremely critical of the manner in which their proposals are scrutinised, modified or amended by the Centre while grants are being sanctioned.

On the other hand, the Centre also is not happy about the situation. It has assumed the role of dominant partner without having any constitutional authority to compel the States to conform to its dictates and without even having a machinery to report on the implementation of its programmes through the State Governments. Its main complaint is that its genuine desire to help the States is misunderstood as interference; that the reasonable minimum safeguards which are and should be adopted in all financial sanctions are misinterpreted as 'indirect pressures' or as 'leading strings'; that the States do not appreciate the larger interests of education underlying the policies and programmes proposed by it; that the States do not often implement the sanctioned schemes in the manner in which they ought to be implemented; and that it often finds itself helpless to enforce the directives given by it. During the last ten years, therefore, education has developed practically into a 'joint responsibility' of the Central and State Governments. But unfortunately, neither partner is satisfied with the present position and each one of them has a number of charges to make against the other. It would be no exaggeration to say that it is this conflict and contradiction in the present position which is at the root of most of our administrative difficulties and it is for the solution of these troubles that the role of the Government of India in education has to be properly defined as early as possible.

In order to pose correctly the complex problems involved in this issue and to arrive at some tentative solutions, it is necessary to consider the problem from three different points of view. The first approach would be historical and it would show how the role of the Government of India in education has varied from time to time and why; the second would start with the analysis of the relevant constitutional provisions and explain what the Constitution expects the Government of India to do in education; and the third would compare and contrast the role of the Government of India in education with that of some other federal governments in the world.

It is only in the light of the findings of these three specific studies that it may finally be possible to draw up some kind of a picture of the role of the Government in education as it ought to be.

7.6 HISTORICAL SURVEY (1773-1950)

From 1773 to 1833.—The Government of India may be said to have been born with the Regulating Act of 1773 which designated the Governor in Council of Bengal as the Governor-General in Council of Bengal and gave him a limited authority over the Governors of Bombay and Madras. This authority was substantially increased by the Pitt's India Act of 1784. But prior to 1833, education in India had made but little progress (it has, in fact, been accepted as a State responsibility only as late as in 1813) and the Governor-General of Bengal did little to control or direct the educational policies of the other parts of India. At this time, therefore, 'education' may be said to have been a 'provincial' matter, subject only to the distant coordinating authority of the Court of Directors in England.

From 1833 to 1870. —The Charter Act of 1833 introduced a unitary system of Government. Under this arrangement, all revenues were raised in the name of the Central Government and all expenditure needed its approval. The Provincial Governments could not spend even one rupee or create a post, however small, without the approval of the Government of India which also was the only law-making body for the country as a whole.

In other words, all executive, financial and legislative authority was exclusively vested in the Central Government and the Provinces merely acted as its agents.

As may easily be imagined, education thus became a purely 'Central' subject in 1833 and the entire authority in education and responsibility for it came to be vested in the Government of India. This excessively centralised system, which became more and more inconvenient as education began to expand and the territories of the Company began to grow, remained in force till 1870. As administrative difficulties began to grow, some small powers were delegated to Provincial Governments from time to time and their proposals, as those of the 'authority on the spot', carried great weight. But the character of the system remained unaltered throughout the period and education continued to be a Central subject in every sense of the term.

From 1870 to 1921.—In 1870, however, Lord Mayo introduced a system of administrative decentralization under which the Provincial Governments were made responsible for all Expenditure on certain services—inclusive of education—and were given, for that purpose, a fixed grant-in-aid and certain sources of revenue. Education thus became a 'provincial subject' for purposes of day-to-day administration. But it has to be remembered that the Central Government still retained large powers of control over it. For instance, both the Central and Provincial Legislatures had concurrent powers to legislate on all educational matters. It was because of this concurrent legislative jurisdiction, that the Government of India could pass the Indian

Universities Act in 1904 and could also legislate for the establishment of new universities. Of the new universities established during this period of British India, only one—Lucknow—was established by an Act of the U.P. Legislature. All others— Punjab (1882), Allahabad (1887), Banaras (1915), Patna (1917), Aligarh (1920) and Dacca (1920) were established by the Central Legislature. It was for the same reason that Gokhale could then introduce his Bill for compulsory Primary education in India in the Central legislature, although it failed to pass. In administrative matters, the sanction of the Government of India was needed to the creation of all new posts above a given salary and in 1897, the Indian Educational Service was created and placed in charge of all the important posts in the Provincial Education Departments. In financial matters, the powers reserved to the Central Government were very wide. Its approval was required to all expenditure above a given figure and to the over-all budget of the Provinces. These large powers of control and supervision were justified on the ground that the Provincial Governments were responsible to the British Parliament through the Government of India. But whatever the cause, the net result of these powers was to make education not so much a 'provincial subject' as a 'concurrent subject' with two reservations: (1) the authority delegated to the Provincial Governments was fairly large; and (2) the interest shown by the Government of India in education was very uneven and depended mostly upon the personalities of the Governor-Generals—a Ripon or a Curzon could make education look almost like a 'Central subject' while, at other times, it became almost a 'provincial subject'.

It must also be noted that the interest and authority of the Government of India was not restricted to any particular field, although it naturally showed very great interest in University education. It appointed the Indian Universities Commission of 1917-19. As stated earlier it passed the Indian Universities Act in 1904 and also incorporated most of the new universities created in this field. It sanctioned large grants-in-aid for the improvement of Secondary and Primary education and for the introduction of science teaching. It also reviewed and laid down policies in such matters as the education of girls, or Anglo-Indians and the establishment of schools of art. The Indian Education Commission of 1882 and the Government Resolutions on Educational Policy issued in 1904 and 1913 covered almost every aspect of education. In short, the view taken in this period was that education is a subject of national importance and that the Government of India must hold itself responsible for the formulation of over-all educational policy; and this view was particularly strengthened in the period between 1900 and 1921 because educational developments were intimately connected with the growth of nation; consciousness and the struggle for Independence. The main function of a federal government in education—to decide national policies in education—was thus clearly understood and accepted during this period.

The need of expert technical advice in education at the Government of India level was also felt during this period and the post of a Director-General of Education—who was to be an educationist and not a civilian and whose duty it was to advise the Government of India on educational matters—was created by Lord Curzon and at the present time, when the very need of an advisory educational service at the Centre is being challenged in certain quarters, it may be well to recall Lord Curzon's defence of the creation of this post :

"My last topic is the desirability of creating a Director General of Education in India. Upon this point I will give my opinions for what they may be worth. To understand the case we must first realise what the existing system and its consequences are. Education is at present a sub-heading of the work of the Home Department, already greatly overstrained. When questions of supreme educational interests are referred to us for decision, we have no expert to guide us, no staff trained to the business, nothing but the precedents recorded in our files to fall back upon. In every other department of scientific knowledge— sanitation, hygiene, forestry, mineralogy, horse-breeding, explosives— the Government possesses expert advisers. In education, the most complex and most momentous of all we have none. We have to rely upon the opinions of officers who are constantly changing, and who may very likely never have had any experience of education in their lives. Let me point to another anamoly. Under the system of decentralisation that has necessarily and, on the whole, rightly be pursued, we have little idea of what is happening in the provinces, until, once every five years, a gentleman comes round, writes for the Government of India the Quinquennial Review, makes all sorts discoveries of which we know nothing and discloses shortcomings which in hot haste we then proceed to redress. How and why this systemless system has been allowed to survive for all these years it passes my wit to determine. Now that we realise it, let us put an end to it forever. I do not desire Imperial Education Department, packed with pedagogues, and crysted with officialism. I do not advocate a Minister or Member of Council for Education. I do not want anything that will turn the Universities into a Department of the State, or fetter the Colleges or Schools with bureaucratic handcuffs. But I do want someone at headquarters who will prevent the Government of India from going wrong, and who will help us to secure that community of principle and of aim without which go drifting about like a deserted bulk on chopping seas. I go further, and say that the appointment of such an officer, provided, that he be himself an expert and an enthusiast, will check the perils of narrowness and pedantry, while his custody of the leading principles of Indian Education will prevent those vagaries of policy and sharp revulsions of action which distract our administration without reforming it. He would not issue orders to the local governments; but he would be to advise the Government of India. Exactly the same want was felt in America, where decentralisation and devotion are even more keenly cherished, and had been carried to greater lengths, than here; and it was met by the creation of a Central Bureau of Education in 1867, which has since then done invaluable work in coordinating the heterogeneous application of common principles. It is for consideration whether such an official in India as I have suggested should, from time to time, summon a representative Committee or Conference, so as to keep in touch with the local jurisdictions, and to harmonise our policy as a whole."*

The creation of this post, and the further creation of a separate Education Department in the Government of India in 1910 and the establishment of a Central Bureau of Education in 1915 made it possible to develop some other federal functions in education. For example, it is the duty of Government of India to collect educational data from the Provinces and to publish periodical reviews on the progress of education in the country - the Clearing House function. The Indian Education Commission (1882) recommended that the Central Government should bring out Quinquennial Reviews on the progress of education in India. Consequently, the first Quinquennial Review on the progress of education in India was published in 1886-87 and subsequent reviews were brought out in 1891-92, 1896-97, 1901-02, 1905-06, 1911-12, 1916-17 and 1921-22. Annual reviews of education were also published from 1913-14 onwards in all years in which the Quinquennial Reviews were not published.

Similarly, it is the duty of a Federal Government to carry out studies in educational problems (as part of its responsibility to provide leadership in educational thought) from time to time and to publish their findings. In particular, it is the responsibility of a Federal Government to study such educational developments in other countries as are likely to be of help in developing education at home. That both these responsibilities were understood, accepted and even fulfilled with a great competence in certain areas, can be seen from the publications issued by the Government of India during this period. Moreover, 'the Government of India also published reports on important events of the period. In short, the research and publications function of the Federal Government was fully accepted and established during the period under review.

The coordinating function of a Federal Government was also recognised during this period. A reference to that has already been made in the speech of Lord Curzon quoted above. It was he who convened the first Conference of the Directors of Public Instruction in India at Simla in 1901. Then started a regular practice of convening such Conferences for taking a periodical review of educational developments. An Educational Conference was held at Allahabad in 1911 and another Conference of the Directors of Public Instruction was held in 1917. With the passage of time, the need for such coordination was felt all the more keenly and a Central Advisory Board of Education was organized in 1920 with a view to assisting the Provincial Governments with expert advice.

Another function of a Federal Government to be recognised during this period was grant of financial assistance for educational development in the Provinces. Reference has already been made to the financial decentralisation introduced by Lord Mayo in 1870. That system continued to be in force up to 1876-77 when a system of 'shared revenues' was introduced.

Under this system, certain revenues were exclusively designated as 'Central', certain others were designated as exclusively 'Provincial'; and the remainder were designated as 'Divided' and their receipts were shared between the Central and Provincial Governments according to an agreed contract which remained in force for a period of five years at a time. Thus the quinquennial contracts were revised in 1882-83, 1886-87, 1891-92 and 1896-97. In 1904, they were declared to be quasi-permanent, i.e., not liable to be changed except in a grave emergency, and in 1912, they were declared as permanent. It will thus be seen that, under these financial arrangements, the entire expenditure on education was to be borne by the Provincial Governments within the resources allocated to them.

As may be easily imagined, these arrangements made the Provincial revenue fairly inelastic and they were unable to keep pace with the rapidly growing commitments of an expanding educational system. The Government of India, therefore, started the practice of giving grants-in-aid to Provincial Governments for educational development over and above the agreed contract arrangements. Thus the fifth important function of the Federal Government, viz., financial assistance, also came to be accepted during this period. Fortunately, the period between 1900 and 1921 was a period of boom in world finances and the Government of India had large surpluses in its budgets. It was, therefore, comparatively easy to allocate a share of these surpluses to the Provincial Governments for expenditure on education. The magnitude of these grants was fairly large and it may also be stated that most of them were specific purpose grants, i.e. the Government of India decided the developmental policies to be adopted and earmarked the grants given for the implementation of specified approved policies. Only a few of these were general grants which were at the disposal of the Provincial Government were they free to spend in any manner they liked.

From 1921 to 1947.—Between 1870 and 1921, therefore, the day-to-day administration of education was delegated to the Provincial Governments and the Government of India continued to function as a Federal Government with five distinct functions, which came to be recognised, viz., the functions of (1) policy-making, (2) clearing house of information, (3) research and publications, (4) coordination and (5) financial assistance.

With the coming into force of the Government of India Act, 1919, however, the position changed completely. The basic idea underlying this Act was that the Government of India should continue to be responsible to the Secretary of State for India that the functions of the Provincial Governments should be divided into two parts— the reserved part being responsible to the Government of India and the transfer being under the control of elected Ministers responsible to the Provincial Legislatures. As a corollary to this decision, it was also agreed that the Government of India have very little or no control over the transferred departments because the Ministers could not be simultaneously responsible to the Government of India as well as to their elected legislatures. These were basic political decisions and it was rather unfortunate that the division of authority in education between the Government of India and the Provincial Governments had to be made on these political considerations and no fundamental educational issues involved. One would have preferred that problems such as the following should have been raised and discussed on this occasion:

- To what extent is education a national problem?
- What should be the role of a Federal Government in education? and
- What should be the relationship between the Government of India and provincial Governments in educational matters?

But, unfortunately, all such basic problems were ignored and the only questions discussed from a political angle were the following: —

- Should education be a transferred subject or not? and
- What should be the control which Government of India should have over education?

The Montagu-Chelmsford Report suggested that the 'guiding principle should be to include in the transferred list those departments which afford most opportunity for local knowledge and social service, those in which Indians have shown themselves to be keenly interested, those in which mistakes which may occur, though serious, would not be irremediable, and those which stand most in need of development.'* In pursuance of this principle, it was but natural to expect that education would be classed as a transferred subject, although one does not feel very happy to be told that mistakes in education are not really very important. It was, therefore, decided that, excepting for the following few reservations, education should be a Provincial subject and transferred to the control of the Indian Ministers:

- The Banaras Hindu University and such other new universities as may be declared to be all-India by the Governor-General-in-Council were excluded on the ground that these institutions were of an all-India character and had better be dealt with by the Government of India itself;

- Colleges for Indian chiefs and educational institutions maintained by the Governor- General-in-Council for the benefit of members of His Majesty's Forces or other public servants, or their children were also excluded on the ground that these institutions ought to be under the direct control of the Government of India; and

- The education of Anglo-Indians and Europeans was treated as a provincial but a reserved subject.

The authority to legislate on the following subjects was reserved for the Central legislature, mainly with a view to enabling the Government of India to take suitable action on the report of the Calcutta University Commission: —

- Questions regarding the establishment, constitution and functions of new universities;

- Questions affecting the jurisdiction of any university outside its province; and

- Questions regarding the Calcutta University and the reorganization of Secondary education in Bengal (for a period of five years only after the introduction of the Reforms).

As a corollary to this decision, it was also decided that the Government of India should have no control over education in the Provinces.

Thus came about what the Hartog Committee has rightly described as the 'divorce' of the Government of India from education. As could easily be imagined, the results were far from happy. The Central interest in education disappeared almost completely after 1921; and when the need for retrenchment arose in 1923, the first victims were (1) the Education Department of the Government of India which lost its independent existence and was amalgamated with other departments, (2) the Central Advisory Board of Education which was dissolved, and (3) the Central Bureau of Education which was closed down. The Central grants to the Provinces for educational development also disappeared, even the few powers of legislation reserved under the Act of 1919 were not exercised, and the Government of India did little beyond the clearing house function of publishing the annual and quinquennial reviews of the progress of education in India.

The Hartog Committee strongly criticised this unhappy position and said:

"We are of opinion that the divorce of the Government of India from education has been unfortunate; and, holding as we do, that education is essentially a national service, we are of opinion that steps should be taken to consider anew the relation of the Central Government with this subject. We have suggested that the Government of India should serve as a centre of educational experience of the different provinces. But we regard the duties of the Central Government as going beyond that. We cannot accept the view that it should be entirely relieved of all responsibility for the attainment of universal primary education. It may be that some of the provinces, in spite of all efforts, will be unable to provide the funds necessary for that purpose, and the Government of India should, therefore, be constitutionally enabled to make good such financial deficiencies in the interests of India as a whole."*

It is also interesting to know that, for some time after 1921, there was an outburst of strong provincial feelings and the divorce of the Government of India from education was even welcomed in some quarters. But it did not take the Provincial Governments long to realise that this was a mistake and that something had to be done to create a national agency and machinery for the development of education. It was, therefore, possible to revise the earlier decision and the Government of India revived the Central Advisory Board of Education in 1935; the Central Bureau of Education was also revived, on a recommendation made by the Central Advisory Board of Education, in 1937; and finally the old Education Department was also revived as a Ministry of Education in 1946. The decisions of 1921 were, therefore, very largely undone by 1947.20. Between 1935 and 1947, therefore, the role of the Government of India in education was again broadened and the several functions which had fallen into disuse between 1923 to 1935 were again resumed. For example, the coordinating function was resumed with great vigour and the Central Advisory Board of Education addressed itself to the study and discussion of almost every field of educational activity and finally prepared, and presented to the nation, a plan for the educational development in India during the next 40 years (1944). The publication function was also resumed and the reconstituted Central Bureau brought out a large number of publications on different aspects of the educational problem in India. The clearing house function was continued and its extent and efficiency were improved. The only functions developed in the earlier period and not resumed now were two—research and financial assistance. In spite of these limitations, however, the larger and more significant role that was now being played by the Government of India was appreciated all over the country; and the general feeling was that this role needed to be further strengthened and extended.

This brief historical survey of the role of the Government of India in education will show that it has passed through a number of stages. Prior to 1833, it had hardly any role to play; between 1833 and 1870, education was virtually a Central subject; between 1870 and 1921, the day-to-day administration was vested in Provincial Governments, but the Government of India discharged five distinct functions, viz., the functions of policy-making, clearinghouse of information, research and publications, coordination and financial assistance; between 1921 and 1935, the wheels of the clock were turned back and there was an almost total divorce between education and the Central Government; but fortunately, more progressive policies were adopted after 1935 and the Government of India began to play, once again, a larger and a more fruitful role in education.

7.7 The Role of the Government of India under the Constitution and in Actual Practice (1950-60)

Soon after the attainment of Independence, the problem of the role of the Government of India in education came up for discussion again when the Constitution was being framed. The thinking of the framers of the Constitution on this subject seems to have been influenced by two main considerations:

(1) The general model adopted in the U.S.A.; and (2) The recommendations of the Hartog Committee. As in the U.S.A., therefore, a fundamental decision was taken to treat education as a State subject and also to vest the residuary powers in education in the State Governments by making a specific enumeration of powers reserved to the Government of India in this field. Entry 11 of List II of the Seventh Schedule to the Constitution, therefore, lays down that "education including universities, subject to the provisions of Entries 63, 64, 65 and 66 of List I and Entry 25 of List III" should be a State subject; and the entries which give authority to the Government of India in education were worded as follows:

List I—Union List

The institutions known at the commencement of this Constitution as the Banaras Hindu University, the Aligarh Muslim University and the Delhi University, and any other institution declared by Parliament by law to be an institution of national importance.

Institutions for scientific and technical education financed by the Government of India wholly or in part and declared by Parliament by law to be institutions of national importance.

Union agencies and institutions for—

- professional, vocational or technical training, including the training of police officers; or
- the promotion of special studies or research; or
- scientific or technical assistance in the investigation or detection of crime.

Co-ordination and determination of standards in institutions for Higher education or research and scientific and technical institutions.

List III—Concurrent List

Vocational and technical training of labour.

In respect of Primary education, however, the Constitution has made an exception on the lines recommended by the Hartog Committee. The intimate relationship between the provision of a minimum of free and compulsory education for all children and the successful working of a democracy which the Constitution decided to create, is obvious. The Constitution, therefore, makes the following provision as a directive principle of State policy under Part IV:

The State shall endeavour to provide within a period of ten years from the commencement of this Constitution, for free and compulsory education for all children until they complete the age of 14 years."

The expression 'State' which occurs in this article is defined in Article 12 to include "the Government and Parliament of India and the

Government and the Legislature of each of the States and all local or other authorities within the territory of India or under the control of the Government of India." The Federal Government is, therefore, under a constitutional obligation to participate in the programme of providing free and compulsory education for all children until they complete the age of 14 years.

Similarly, the Constitution also makes it an obligatory responsibility of the Government of India to promote the educational interest of the weaker sections of the people and makes the following provision:

The State shall promote with special care the educational and economic interests of the weaker sections of the people, and, in particular, of the Scheduled Castes and the Scheduled Tribes, and shall protect them from social injustice and all forms of exploitation."

The expression "weaker sections of the people", as used in this article, is general and is not restricted to the Scheduled Castes and the Scheduled Tribes only. For example, it will obviously include women and consequently the development of the education of girls and women becomes a special responsibility of the Government of India. In the same way, the expression also means people living in those areas where economic and cultural development lags behind. This article, therefore, makes it a responsibility of the Government of India to bring about an equalisation of educational opportunities in all parts of the country and, to that end, to give special assistance to the backward areas or States.

There is yet another provision in the Constitution which has an indirect but significant bearing upon the role of Government of India in education. Entry in the List III is "Economic and Social Planning" and this implies that the Government of India has a consititutional responsibility for the economic and social development of the country as a whole. Now, it is a well-known sociological principle that economic and social development is intimately connected with education and it is in this sense that the White Paper on Education in the United Kingdom said : "Upon the education given to the children of this country, the future of this country depends." It is function of the schools to define the objectives of a national economic and social planning although they can, and should, to some extent, direct and influence their definition. But once the objectives of economic and social planning are decided upon by the powers that be, education has a very important role to play in assisting the nation to realise these objectives. For instance, the schools will never be able to decide whether democracy should or should not be a national way of life, whether socialism should or should not be accepted or whether rapid industrialisation should or should not be resorted to. But if the nation were to decide to accept these goals, education will help very greatly in creating and stabilising a social order based on these values by developing the necessary aptitudes, skills and interests in the rising generation. As Brubacher has observed, "schools can complete and consolidate a change decided elsewhere—whether by bullets or by ballots." The implication is obvious: an authority like the Government of India which is responsible for the economic and social planning of the country, cannot divest itself of a major responsibility in determining corresponding educational policies to realise its economic and social objectives. In spite of the limited direct authority which the Constitution gives to the Government of India, therefore, practices have actually grown up, as a part of the formulation and implementation of the Five Year Plans of the country, under which the major educational policies are being decided; more at the Centre than in the States and the distribution of resources to education in general for the different sectors of education in particular, is becoming more a matter for a decision at the Central level than at the State levels.

On a very close examination of all the provisions of the Constitution which have a bearing on education, one cannot help the feeling that there is an element of basic contradiction in the role which the Constitution attempts to assign to the Goverment of India in education. On the one hand, the Constitution takes the simple stand that education, with all residuary powers, is a state subject except for a few special aspects specified within the Constitution itself. But the real trouble starts when the enumeration of these 'exceptions' begins. For instance, free and compulsory education is made an obvious exception on account of its cost and significance and Centre is given a specific responsibility for it (Art 45).

Similarly, the responsibility of the Centre to equalise educational opportunities between different areas or different sections of society had also to be recognised and duly provided for (Art. 46). Then the responsibility of the Centre to safeguard the cultural interests of the minority and to see that they have adequate facilities to receive at least primary education through their own mother-tongue (Art. 350 A) as well as the special responsibility of the Centre to develop the national language (Art. 351) had also to be provided for. The need for controlled development of Higher education made it necessary to authorize the Centre to coordinate and determine standards in universities and scientific, technical, or research institutions (Entry 66 of List I) and, on account of such factors as high cost, difficulty of securing suitable personnel, the need to obtain foreign assistance, etc. Scientific research, technical education, and the higher types of professional and vocational education had also to be assigned to the Centre (Entries 64 and 65 of List I). Certain educational problems which have a large significance at present such as securing of foreign assistance (in men, materials or money) for education, training of Indians abroad, relationship with international organisations like UNESCO, participation in bilateral or multi-lateral programmes of educational assistance like the Commonwealth Cooperation Scheme or the T. C. M. had also to be left to the Centre under Entries 10 and 12 of List I. Finally, a very powerful means of central control was created when 'Economic and Social Planning' was made a concurrent responsibility (Entry 20 of List III). These exceptions are so large that they circumscribe the State authority for education very materially and make education look more like a 'joint' responsibility than like a State preserve. But this is not all. It has to be remembered that the Constitution was out to create a 'strong' Centre. It has, therefore, rested most of the important resources in the Government of India and the result is that no State has adequate resources of its own to develop education—the costliest of welfare services. Consequently the Centre, which controls the purse-strings, necessarily has the most dominating voice in the overall determination of policies, priorities and programmes. From this point of view, therefore, education begins to look, not only as a joint responsibility, but almost like a 'partnership' in which the Government of India plays the role of the 'Big Brother'. This implied constitutional role of the Government of India in education, therefore, is directly opposed to the explicit role as stated in Entry 11 of List II; and it is this basic contradiction inherent in the Constitutional provisions that leads to most of the controversies on the subject.

The situation is further complicated by another consideration. The role of a federal government in education is determined, not so much by the provisions of the Constitution as by conventions and practices evolved through historical developments. Perhaps the finest example of this is the Constitution of the U. S. A. itself. As is well-known, the tradition of local control in education is extremely strong in the U. S. A. and both in history and in law, education is specifically a State subject. The country has consequently developed a highly decentralized system of educational administration and it is worthy of note that the federal constitution does not even contain a reference to 'schools' or 'education'. All these factors should tend to make the role of the U. S. federal government in education extremely weak.

But the facts are that federal aid to education is older than the federal constitution; and the present functions and responsibilities of the U. S. federal government in education are far heavier and more important than in several other countries where even the Constitution makes the federal government responsible for education in some way or the other. Today the U. S. Federal Government conducts a U. S. Office of Education which serves as a clearing house of ideas and information. It is also directly responsible for a number of educational programmes such as education for national defence (inclusive of the programme of the schooling of the veterans of the second World War), cooperation with other nations in a world-wide educational endeavour, in education in union territories and the education of the children of federal employees residing in government reservations, in dependencies and at foreign stations. Almost "every branch of the federal government conducts several educational activities. . . Congress has its Committees on education in both the House and the Senate. The Supreme Court renders its interpretations in the form of decisions, as in the Dartmouth College Case, the MacCollum and Zorach decisions on public schools and religious instruction, the opinions on segregations in schools and colleges, and the interpretations on loyalty legislation affecting educators. Independent federal establishments

that furnish educational service include the library of the Congress and its Copyright Office, the Government Printing Office, the Pan-American Union, the Smithsonian Institution, the National Museum, the National Gallery of Art, the National Academy of Sciences, the Commission of Fine Arts, the Atomic Energy Commission and the National Science Foundation. Much educational research is conducted in the Nation's Capital and sponsored by the Congress of the United States". In times of national crises, such as the depression of the 1930's, the federal government assisted a number of emergency programmes such as the Civilian Conservation Corps (CCC), National Youth Administration (NYA) Works Progress Administration (WPA), and other agencies. It has also assumed certain responsibilities for the education of backward groups like the Red Indians or Negroes. But above all, it has made large funds available for educational development without any idea of imposing federal control in education. As stated above, this tradition of federal financial assistance' without 'federal control' is very old and goes back to 1785 while the Constitution itself was ratified in 1788. The first grants to education were in terms of land, but very soon money grants were also introduced.

The purposes for which federal grants were or are being given include: (1) agricultural education through the development of land-grant colleges with experimental farms and extension services attached; (2) vocational education in Secondary schools; (3) vocational training in distributed occupations; (4) vocational rehabilitation of the handicapped; (5) vocational guidance and placement; etc. All this, it must be said, is being done when the Constitution does not refer to education at all and the legal basis of all this huge and significant activity is the 'general welfare' clause in the Constitution. Hardly any other proof is needed to show that it is the historical background, and not the explicit provisions of the Constitution, that ordinarily determine the actual role of a federal government in education.

Assuming this thesis for the sake of argument, the relevant question is: what have been the developments in Indian education since the adoption of the Constitution and how have they affected the constitutional roles of the Government of India and the State Governments in defining and implementing educational policies? In this context, attention may be specially invited to three significant developments. The first is the growing desire to evolve a national system of education for the country as a whole. This desire found an expression as early as 1906 when the Surat Congress passed a resolution on national education. It was given a great fillip by Mahatma Gandhi in his Non Cooperation Movement of 1921. But at this time, the idea was mainly restricted to few non-official agencies. When the popular Ministries came to power in 1937, the movement also assumed an official form and an attempt was now made to reorient all educational institutions to the concept of national education. This desire naturally became even stronger when popular Governments came to power both in the Centre and the States.

Such a desire obviously implies the assumption of a leading role in the formulation and implementation of educational programmes by the Government of India. The same implication has been further strengthened by the growing realization of the fact that education has a national significance, that it would be almost fatal to the future of the nation to treat it as purely local, that a group of States each of whom is sovereign to decide its own educational policies may even do more harm than good to national solidarity, and that a Central agency to coordinate and develop a national system of education is inevitable in the present conditions when education is generally backward in all parts of the country and very unevenly developed in its different parts. It is this realisation of the national significance of education and the growing desire to create a national system of education that have led to the unprecedented activity of the Government of India in education during the last ten years and, to that extent, diminished the constitutional responsibility of the States for education.

A second development of the period which has also helped to give the Government of India a dominant voice in the formulation of educational policies is the revival of central grants for education to which a reference has already been made. This revival was of course inevitable in the financial and administrative set-up created by the constitution which vests all the best resources in the Centre and makes the States responsible for all the expensive social services.

If the surplus resources at the Centre could have been passed to the needy States with little or no controls, the responsibility of the States for the development of education would have been strengthened. But this did not happen. The attempts of the Centre in policy-making often got mixed up with its attempts at financial assistance and thus arose the charge that Central grants are being used as levers to secure acceptance of Central educational policies. That this charge is largely unfounded will be shown later; but one result of the large Central grants for education has to be admitted: they created a situation in which a very large part of the funds needed for educational development came from the Centre through grant-in-aid. Consequently, the States have tended to lose their spirit of self-reliance and self-confidence and are developing a habit of looking up to Delhi for almost everything.

The third development of this period which undermined the responsibility of the States for education and this was a development which has done the greatest damage in this sector—came from outside the educational field, viz., the adoption of centralized planning and the creation of the Planning Commission. In the new technique of planning that has now been adopted, more and more decisions tend to be taken at the Centre than in the States. The decision on national targets, the fixation of priorities, the allocation of resources to different sectors of development or even to different programmes within the same sector of development, the allocation of resources to different States, the fixation of the Central assistance to each State—these and such other problems are mainly decided by the Planning Commission and all these affect educational policies so largely that a State Government is very often required, not to prepare an educational plan, but to fill in the blanks or details of a structure whose broad irrevocable outline has already been decided elsewhere. Even the Ministry of Education finds itself in the same weak predicament as the States visa-a-visa the Planning Commission. It is these developments that have contributed most to the trend to centralization in education during the last ten years and it is because of them that the responsibility of States for education has been most weakened.

It will thus be seen that the inherent contradiction in the constitutional position has been still further accentuated by the developments of the last ten years and the role of the Centre has now become far more important in actual practice than in the cold print of the Constitution. It must also be remembered that these developments are not necessarily deplored. They are, in fact, welcomed in several quarters and today, a strong section of opinion in the country favours a proposal to amend the Constitution and to make education a concurrent subject. The lack of adequate leadership which is sometimes conspicuous at the State level and the frequently noticed distortion of State educational policies under immediately political or parochial pressures also tend to emphasize and strengthen this viewpoint.

This equivocal position has given rise to a bitter controversy regarding the correct role of the federal government in education; and as suggested in the opening paragraphs, this problem will have to be satisfactorily solved at an early date.

7.8 THE ROLE OF THE FEDERAL GOVERNMENT IN EDUCATION—A COMPARATIVE STUDY (AUSTRALIA, CANADA, THE U. S. A. AND THE U. S. S. R.)

The main object of this paper is to discuss the role of the Government of India in education as it ought to be. But before taking up this issue, it would be of advantage to make a brief comparative study of the role of the federal government in education in four selected countries—Australia, Canada, the U.S.A. and the U.S.S.R.

Australia. Of all the countries mentioned above, Australia is an example of the weakest role that a federal government can ever play in education. The reasons for this peculiar situation are purely historical. The States of Australia were founded and grew as independent colonies and it was only as late as in 1901 that the federal government was created. By this time, every State had developed its own educational system and such a strong local sentiment and tradition for education had been created that the people did not think it necessary to invest the federal government with any authority in education. Nay, there was even a feeling that federal control and intervention in education would do great harm; and this explains why the Australian Constitution makes no reference to education and why the federal government took no steps for educational development for several years after its formation. The Australian Council for Educational Research began as a voluntary enterprise with a grant from the Carnegie Foundation; and the first attempts to form a federal agency in education were restricted to periodical meetings of the Directors and Ministers of Education of all the States for the discussion of common problems. In 1943, a Universities Commission was established and its functions were defined as follows: (a) to arrange for the training of ex-soldiers in universities or similar institutions; (b) to assist students studying in universities or similar institutions; (c) to advise the Minister with respect to such matters relating to university training and associated matters as are referred to it by the Minister for advice; and (d) to assist other persons, in prescribed cases or classes of cases, to obtain training in universities or similar institutions. It is easy to see that this Universities Commission is quite different from the Indian University Grants Commission. In 1945, the Commonwealth Office of Education was established and its functions were listed as follows: (a) to advise the Minister on matters relating to education; (b) to establish and maintain liaison on matters relating to education, with other countries and with the States; (c) to arrange consultation between Commonwealth authorities concerned with matters relating to education; (d) to undertake research relating to education; (e) to provide statistics and information relating to education required by any Commonwealth authority; (f) to advise the Minister concerning the grant of financial assistance to the States and the other authorities for educational purposes; and (g) such other functions in relation to education as are assigned to it by the Minister.

In spite of the general attitude to keep the federal government out of education as far as possible, certain educational functions had to be taken up. For instance, responsibilities for scientific and industrial research had to be assumed by the federal government and the Commonwealth Scientific and Industrial Research Organisation was set up with the object of placing "at the service of producers throughout Australia, both in primary and secondary industries, the highest ability and the most advanced knowledge in order to reduce the cost and increase the volume of production". As a further development of the same trend, the National Australian University was established at Canberra in 1948. It has been empowered to establish research schools, including a School of Medical Research, a Research School of Physical

Science, a Research School of Social Science, and a Research School of Pacific Studies. The University is exclusively engaged in research and the benefit of its work extends to the whole of Australia and all the countries and Island of the Pacific. Similarly, the federal government has had to assume responsibility for the education of the Maoris. It has also established one model pre-school centre in each State capital and has taken upon itself the responsibility to organise a National Fitness programme.

Some explanation is needed about the power of the federal government to give financial assistance. In the first place, the federal government in Australia has the sole power to levy major taxes and the proceeds are distributed to the States on some general principles which have no relationship with the scale of State expenditures. These financial allocations cannot, therefore, be described as 'grants' or 'assistance' in the proper sense of the term. But off and on, the federal government does give grants for some educational purposes from its own resources. For example, grants were given for the establishment of a School for Aeronautical Engineering in the University of Melbourne and a School of Public Health and Tropical Medicine in the University of Sydney. As an aid to the National Fitness programme, the State Grants (Milk for School Children) Act was passed in 1950 and provision was made for supply of milk to children under 13. The scheme is to be administered by the States and the expenditure is to be reimbursed by the federal government.

Canada. The role of the Canadian Federal Government in education is similar to that in Australia with two major differences: (1) the problem of linguistic and religious minorities is acute in Canada and needs special safeguards, and (2) it is more influenced by the developments in the U.S.A.

As is well-known, the present Dominion of Canada arose out of a fusion of British and French colonies. The French-speaking people who are mostly Roman Catholics are a minority in the Dominion as a whole but a majority in certain parts such as Quebec and the position of the English-speaking people, who are mostly Protestants, is just the opposite of this. Special safeguards for the interests of minorities had, therefore, to be provided in the federal constitution—the British North America Act of 1867—which lays down that the educational rights enjoyed by the religious minorities prior to their entry into the Dominion shall not be abrogated and, in cases of dispute, provides appeals to the Governor-General-in-Council and to the Privy Council in London. Safeguarding the educational rights of minorities is thus an essential federal responsibility in Canada.

The federal government in Canada is also constitutionally responsible for the education in the territories, for the education of Red Indians and Eskimos, and for training for national defence.

As in Australia, scientific and other research has become a federal responsibility and the "National Research Council, in conjunction with the national research laboratories in Ottawa, maintains laboratories, offers scholarships to research students, and pays grants-in-aid for investigations conducted at the University level by Provincial Departments of Education". As in the U.S.A., Canada also has made large land and money grants for education and assists programmes of vocational and technical education in schools. There is, however, no Federal Ministry or Department of Education, not even an Office of Education as in the U.S.A. or Australia. There is a Dominion Bureau of Statistics which publishes, as one of its multifarious duties, an Annual Survey of Education in Canada. There is also a Canadian Education Association which collects and publishes research studies and generally functions as a clearing house for information and ideas. Recently, the federal government has given financial assistance for increasing staff salaries in universities and it also bears the expenditure on school broadcasts. All things considered, therefore, the general opinion is "that the part played in education by the Dominion Government in Canada is important, but neither extensive nor expending".

The U.S.A.—A reference has already been made in paragraph 25 to the different activities of the US Federal Government in education and it is, therefore, only necessary to refer briefly here to the modern trends in the US education which will ultimately result in a substantial increase in the federal participation in educational development.

One of the most important modern trends of thinking in the USA is that education is also a national responsibility and that, whatever justification there may have been for leaving it exclusively to the States in 1788 when the Constitution was framed, the entire position has to be examined afresh in the light of present day requirements. In fact, it is readily pointed out that the position of exclusive State responsibility for education adopted in 1788 has already become obsolete and that the federal government has, during the last hundred and seventy years, developed a number of very significant and large-scale educational functions to meet the demands of changing times. The most pointed example of this is the recent federal effort to scout for talent in scientific studies and to improve science education when it was realised that the USSR was probably outstripping the USA in the development of science; and all that is now urged is that the federal role in education will have to be expanded still further if the USA has to hold her own in the modern world.

Assuming that the federal government shall expand its educational activities, the direction in which this expansion should take place is the next important issue to be discussed in this field. One important area suggested is federal grants for 'general education'—which corresponds to the free and compulsory education visualised in Article 45 of the Indian Constitution—with a view to 'equalising educational opportunities'. In no country of the world has so much research and study been carried out on this problem as in the USA. The work really started with a study of educational facilities provided by the local communities on whom, not very long ago, the entire responsibility for general education was made to rest. It was discovered that the 'educational load' of communities, as shown by the number of children to be educated, varied largely from place to place—rural and agricultural districts generally had more children per 1000 of population than urban and industrialised districts. Secondly, the 'ability' of the communities to support education, as measured by their taxable capacity also showed large variations and very often, a community with a poor 'ability' to support education was required to carry larger 'educational load'. Thirdly, the 'effort' of the community for education, as measured by the percentage of its taxable capacity raised and devoted to education, also showed large variations; and finally, the educational 'achievements' of the different communities showed extreme variations—some communities providing a very high standard of education to all the children, while others could neither enrol all children nor maintain adequate standards in schools. What is worse, it was found that several communities made the greatest 'effort' to provide education and yet, either because of poor 'capacity' or heavy 'educational loads' or both, they could only show a poor standard of 'achievement'. Such disparities are increased rather than decreased by the system of 'matching grants' which give more to the rich than to the poor. To remove all these shortcomings and to provide equality of educational opportunity for all children, which is a fundamental need of democracy, the State Governments have given up the idea of grants-in aid on the basis of matching funds alone and have supplemented it by a new system of grant in- aid on the basis of equalization. The process is complicated but it works out somewhat on the following lines: In the first instance, the State prescribes what is called a 'foundation programme' that is to say, a minimum programme below which no community can be allowed to fall. The programme includes targets for enrolments, teachers' salaries, school buildings, provision of health services (inclusive of school meals) and other contingent expenditures so that it is both a qualitative and a quantitative programme. The second step in the process is to work out the total cost of this programme for each community; and the third step is to determine the 'reasonable' effort which the local community is expected to make. The difference between the total cost of the foundation programme and the reasonable effort expected of the community.

These ideas which have now come to stay at the community level are being naturally extended to the State level and studies made so far have shown that the States themselves exhibit wide variation in 'educational loads', in 'abilities', in 'efforts' to support education and in 'achievements'. Consequently, a demand is now being put forward to the effect that 'equalization of educational opportunity' must be accepted as a Federal responsibility. The federal government, it is said, must lay down a minimum foundation programme for all States and must give equalisation grants where necessary on principles similar to those mentioned above. It is also evident that the support for this concept of federal aid to education is rapidly gaining ground and that it is only a matter of time when federal grants for equalisation of educational opportunities would be generally available.

The main argument against this wholesome and urgent reform is the fear that federal aid to education will necessarily be followed by federal control. There are several thinkers who would rather refuse federal aid than have federal control. But an equally strong argument is now being put forward that federal aid can and should be given without federal control.

"According to many fiscal experts," writes De Young, "no sound programme of local or state taxation can be devised and established which will support in every community a school system that meets minimum acceptable standards. Time can never efface the inequalities in natural resources that exist between states. Therefore, unless the federal government participates in the financial support of the schools and the related services the less able areas, several million children in the United States and the outlying territories and possessions will continue to be denied the educational opportunities that should be regarded as their birthright. Most recommendations and recent proposals for federal aid stipulate positively that such grants shall not entail federal control over education. They also specify that the money shall be apportioned to the states, except that for cooperative educational research, which shall be administered by the United States Office of Education. Several decades ago Rutherford B. Hayes, then President of the United States, sent to Congress a message in which he said: "No more fundamental responsibility rests upon Congress than that of devising appropriate measures of financial aid to education, supplemental to local action in the states and territories and in the District of Columbia. This challenge has not yet been adequately met. Federal aid to public education is one of the moral 'musts' of America."

Apart from this major 'equalisation' aid for general education, the following programmes have also been suggested for federal assistance:

- Scholarships and Fellowships in Higher education to be made available to undergraduate, graduate and professional students (scheme to be administered by the States);
- Scholarships for talented youth in Secondary Schools;
- Improvement of teacher education; and
- Educational experimentation and pilot projects.

The U.S.S.R.—The three examples given so far are those of countries which have accepted democracy as a way of life and which also have a federal form of government. The U.S.S.R., on the other hand, is a totalitarian state with a federal form of government and it would be interesting to compare the role of the federal government in education under such a system. There is no federal Ministry of Education in the U.S.S.R. and this may lead one to suppose that the Soviet Union has a decentralized system of education. Nothing can be farther from the truth; and in no country of the world is education so rigidly controlled by a central authority as in the U.S.S.R. This paradox, therefore, needs some explanation and it can be understood only in terms of Soviet philosophy and administrative techniques.

Under communist philosophy, the most important objective in education is to create the "new Soviet Man" which means a person who is fully imbued with the philosophy of communism and who becomes an efficient and loyal worker of the State in the field to which he may be ultimately assigned. In the Soviet system, therefore, the highest significance is attached to the control of the contents of education and of all the media which influence the thinking of men such as films, radio, television, concert-hall, the theatre, press, books, lecture platform, etc. The determination of the contents of education and the control of all media of communication in such a manner as to produce the one effect desired on the minds of all men becomes, therefore, a responsibility of the highest Soviet authority. It is the authorities at the federal level, therefore, that determine the curricula and methods of instruction to ensure that education is in line with Party and State Policy. Once decided, these curricula and methods are adopted in every school in order that a uniform education could be planned and implemented for the nation as a whole. All the different agencies that administer education at lower levels—from the State to the local Soviet—have no control over these fundamental issues and their main responsibility is to provide the necessary facilities to give effect to these Central decisions.

Secondly, the communist philosophy attaches the highest significance to the provision of free and compulsory education for every child and for the provision of Higher education to every gifted child according to his capacity because it is only under such a system that the new Soviet Man can be created. In the planned and centralized economy of the U.S.S.R., therefore, all the necessary funds required for the educational programme are provided from the common financial pool and then allocated to the different subordinate units. In other words, the federal financial resources of the U.S.S.R. are fully pledged for the support of education and for ensuring equality of educational opportunity for all.

It has also to be remembered that the U.S.S.R. is an example of educational control by a single

Party. Speaking from a purely technical point of view, it is possible to describe the different levels In Soviet educational administration to which specific functions have been allocated by law. But as the Communist Party alone controls every administrative unit from the lowest to the highest, the entire control of education is centralized in the Communist Party and delegations of administrative authority to lower levels makes no difference in this respect.

Subject to these three general observations in which the situation in the U.S.S.R. is not strictly comparable to other countries, the role of the U.S.S.R. federal government in education may be stated as follows :—

- There is a Union-Republic Ministry of Higher Education in Moscow (known briefly as the RSFSR Ministry of Higher Education). It exercises supervisory control, including control of general academic standards over all Soviet Higher educational institutions and semiprofessional schools. It controls teaching staff, curricula, textbooks, enrolment quotas and the assignment of graduates. The Soviet Universities have no autonomy as we understand it—they are merely departments of the State.

- The RSFSR Ministry of Higher Education is also charged with the task of anticipating and meeting all needs for man-power in the USSR. In the planned economy that the USSR is trying to build up, it is of the highest importance to train the manpower and to discover the new techniques required for the expanding economy and it is, therefore, an important objective of Soviet Higher education to prepare qualified specialists for all branches of national economy and culture. A very elaborate procedure has also been evolved to discharge this responsibility. Each Ministry works out its requirements of personnel in precise detail and these form an integral part of its development plan. When the national plan is finalised, therefore, it also includes the total requirements of man-power of all categories and it becomes the main object of the educational plan to train and supply this personnel. This most significant task, as stated above, is mainly entrusted to the RSFSR Ministry of Higher Education.

- The RSFSR Ministry of Higher Education also conducts an Academy of Pedagogical Sciences and through it, takes a lead in formulating standard study programmes, working out new procedures, setting up criteria for academic attainment, conducting educational experiments or broadcasting their results, etc.

- At the federal level, there is also a RSFSR Ministry of Culture which deals mainly with cultural-educational establishments for adults including those concerned with music, art, drama, movies, ballet, public libraries and lectures, houses of culture, museums, rural clubs, etc. In the democratic countries, recreation is a purely private enterprise. In the USSR, it becomes, in keeping with the communist philosophy, a controlled and significant activity of the State and both its content and method, like those of education, are severely controlled from the federal level.

- (e) The USSR federal government also performs the usual non-controversial functions assigned to this level, such as (1) collection of statistics and data and (2) arranging for consultations between State Ministries of Education and co-ordinating their activities.

But as may easily be imagined, these consultations do not have much significance. The most effective discussions in policy-making take place at Communist Party Congresses and "resolutions having significance for the general educational development of the whole country are promulgated by the Supreme Soviet of the USSR and the USSR Council of Ministers. Such decrees specify, inter alia, the types of schools to be established, basic organisation, academic programmes to be followed and general provisions regarding compulsory education".

There are, it is true, a number of other federations in the world. But a detailed examination of education in all or even some of them is not very essential to this study. The four States examined here illustrate all the important issues involved and the study of other federations would only repeat them in various combinations.

The foregoing studies show, apart from the general characteristics of federal functions in education and the manner of implementing them, a few other interesting principles useful to an examination of the problem under review. To begin with it may be said that Australia stands at one end of the ladder as having the weakest role in education while the USSR stands at the other as having the strongest one while intermediate positions are occupied, in order of an increasingly important role, by Canada and the USA. India, it may be noticed, stands somewhere between the USA and the USSR. Having accepted democracy as a way of life, it would not centralise education under the federal government as has been done in the USSR.

The Constitution, therefore, had to adopt a model more in keeping with democratic traditions and it is not surprising that the model of the USA where education is a State subject was selected for the purpose. But no country can solve its problems by mere imitation and the general model of the USA had to be modified on account of three reasons: (1) The American Constitution provides for strong State Governments with residuary powers vested in the States while the Indian Constitution wanted to create a strong Centre with residuary powers vested in the Centre; (2) Education in the USA is fully developed and the States are doing so much for it and so well that the need of federal action does not arise in most matters, while in India education has yet to be developed and the States would not be able to do so unless the Centre played a more prominent role of leadership and assistance; and (3) Allowance had to be made for the conditions peculiar to India and for the fact that the role of the federal government in the USA itself was expanding in certain directions which it would be very advantageous for India to copy. These basic considerations, which appear to have led the framers of the Constitution to deviate from the USA model and to endow the

Indian federation with more powers and responsibilities in education, are still applicable and it is quite clear that, in the ultimate solution of the problem, India will be found to be holding a position intermediate between the USA and the USSR.

7.9 THE ROLE OF THE GOVERNMENT OF INDIA IN EDUCATION— AS IT IS AND AS IT OUGHT TO BE

In view of the studies made in the preceding sections—the historical study in Part II and the comparative study in Part IV—it is now possible to take up the thread of the argument where it was left in Part III—the analysis of the contradictions and conflicts in the existing educational role of the Government of India—and to discuss how this role could be reorganised in the near future.

When one examines the role which the Constitution assigns to the federal government in education (or the role which it has now come to play in actual practice) and compares it with the role which other federal governments play in education, or even with the role which the Government of India itself played in the earlier years of our history, one can easily conclude that the following activities may be undoubtedly regarded as "federal functions in education":

1. Educational and cultural relations with other countries;

2. The clearing house function of collecting and broadcasting ideas and information;

3. The coordinating function of harmonizing the educational activities of the Centre and the States;

4. Education in the Union Territories;

5.   Scientific research;

6.   Technical education;

7.   Propagation, development and enrichment of Hindi;

8.   Preservation and promotion of national culture inclusive of patronage to national art;

9.   Patronage to the study of ancient Indian culture in general and the study of Sanskrit in particular;

10.   Education of the handicapped;

11.   Promotion and coordination of educational research;

12.   Special responsibility for the cultural interests of the minorities;

13.   Responsibility for the weaker sections of the people i.e. the Scheduled Castes and Scheduled Tribes;

14.   Responsibility for strengthening national unity through suitable programmes and particularly through those of emotional integration;

15.   Grant of scholarships in an attempt to scout for talent, especially at the University stage;

16.   Advanced professional and vocational training; and

17.   Maintenance of Central Institutions or agencies for education; and

18.   Provision of free and compulsory education up to the age of 14 years.

These eighteen functions may be broadly divided into two groups—the exclusive and the concurrent. The first four functions obviously fall in the 'exclusive' group since no State Government can perform them. The remaining fourteen functions fall into the 'concurrent' group in the sense that every State Government will have to participate in these programmes both on its own initiative and as an agent of the Government of India; but the over-all responsibility for these matters whose national significance is universally recognised would be on the Government of India.

'A few explanatory remarks are perhaps necessary in support of the federal character of these eleven functions. In so far as scientific research and technical education (the fifth and sixth functions), are concerned, it may be stated that they have been accepted as federal functions everywhere. In India, the Federal responsibility for them is far more significant at the present moment, partly because scientific and Technical education is not adequately developed in the States and partly because a good deal of finance and technical help is being made available by a number of advanced countries to assist educational progress in India. The seventh function, viz., the development of Hindi, the national language, is naturally a peculiar and special responsibility of the Government of India. It has hardly any parallels in the western world; but a similar problem has to be faced in Asiatic countries with a multi-lingual population such as Malaya or Philippines. The eighth function, viz., the preservation and promotion of national culture, inclusive of patronage to national art, is an important federal function in almost all the countries. In India also, this function was assumed fairly early and its significance has increased very largely in the post-

Independence period owing to the disappearance of the Indian Princely order which was well known for its patronage to art. The ninth function, viz., the study of ancient Indian culture in general and that of Sanskrit in particular, also becomes a federal responsibility in India. These studies, which have no immediate utilitarian value, are likely to be pushed to the background in the stress of present day demands and it is, therefore, a duty of the federal government to conserve this heritage of centuries and to pass it on to the successive generations as a source of inspiration.

The Government of India has also had to assume some responsibilities for the education of handicapped children, the tenth function. This is both a philosophic and a practical need. The handicapped children are 'a weaker section of the people' and their education and economic improvement thus becomes a responsibility of the federal government also under Article 46 of the Constitution; and even from the strictly practical point of view, it would not be feasible and financially worthwhile for every State Government to provide the necessary trained personnel and costly equipment required for the purpose. The decision of the Government of India to enter this field to do some pioneer work and to assist the State Governments and the voluntary organisations working for this cause has, therefore, been generally welcomed. In fact the demand is for a much larger expansion of the federal activities in this sector than what is visualised at present.

The eleventh function, viz., the promotion and coordination of educational research is a federal function in Australia and the U.S.S.R. but not in the U.S.A. or Canada where well-organised non-official agencies attend to it. But in the peculiar conditions of India at present, this has to be a federal function. Hardly any effort has been made so far to set up Research Bureau in the State Education Departments or to develop strong centres for research in the training colleges or University Departments of Education. Very little has been done to collect data on the research that is going on and still less of it is being published. There is not a single journal in the country devoted to educational research and hardly any measures are being taken to count for research talent and to develop research techniques in education. Since the formulation of correct and progressive policies depends very largely on the development of research, it goes without saying that this function would have to receive much more attention in the near future than it has ever had in the past and that early measures will have to be taken to remedy all the deficiencies pointed out above. It is only a vigorous central action in this sector that can achieve these objectives.

With regard to the twelfth function, viz., the special responsibility for the cultural interests of the minorities, reference has already been made to the Canadian Constitution where the federal government is specially charged with the responsibility of protecting the educational and cultural interests of the minorities. In India, the position is even more difficult than in Canada which has to deal with only two sub-sects of a religion and only two languages. The protection of the cultural and educational interests of the minorities is, therefore, a very important responsibility of the Government of India and the success of our democracy will very largely depend upon the extent and the manner in which this function is discharged and confidence is created in the minds of the minorities concerned.

The Constitution already provides certain safeguards for the cultural and educational interests of minorities. For instance, Article 29(1) guarantees that any section of the citizens having a distinct language, script or culture of its own shall have the right to conserve the same. Article 30(1) gives the minorities, whether based on religion or language, the right to establish and administer educational institutions of their choice, and clause (2) of the same

Article further provides that such institutions shall not be discriminated against in respect of grant-in-aid on the only ground that they are under the management of a minority. Article 29(2) provides that no citizen shall be denied admission into any educational institution maintained by the State or receiving aid out of State funds on grounds only of religion, race, caste, language or any of them. Article 350A directs that it shall be the endeavour of every State and every local authority to provide adequate facilities for instruction in the mother tongue at the Primary stage of education to children belonging to linguistic minority groups; and Article 350B provides for the appointment of a Special Officer for linguistic minorities with the specific object of investigating into all matters relating to safeguards provided for linguistic minorities under the Constitution.

While these provisions are generally welcomed, a common criticism is that they are not adequate and that some additional measures are necessary. For instance, it has been suggested that the educational institutions conducted by linguistic minorities at the Primary stage of education should have a right to receive grant-in-aid from State funds, at least to the extent of the expenditure per pupil incurred by the State Government concerned for its own primary schools. It has also been claimed that the educational interests of the linguistic minorities at other stages of education need some special consideration which is not given at present. It has further been suggested that it is the responsibility of the Government of India to maintain, in all parts of the country, a sufficient number of institutions of Higher education teaching through the medium of Hindi or English in order to provide for the educational interests of the children of its own employees who are liable to be transferred to any part of the Union and also for the legitimate protection of the educational interests of small and scattered linguistic minorities. The whole problem is delicate and difficult and it is not possible to suggest any simple and clearcut solution to it, but the need for the exercise of vigilance by the federal government in this regard is obvious.

The thirteenth function refers to the federal responsibility for the education of Scheduled Castes and Scheduled Tribes. Under Article 46 of the Constitution, the Government of India is responsible for the economic and educational development of the Scheduled Castes and Scheduled Tribes and, as has been pointed out earlier, similar responsibilities have been adopted by other federal governments also—the Federal Government in the U.S.A. having special responsibility for Red Indians and Negroes, in Australia for Maoris and in Canada for Red Indians and Eskimos. Under the present set-up, this responsibility has been vested in the Ministry of Home Affairs which is assisted, in its turn, by all the Ministries of the Government of India, wherever necessary. The Ministry of Education has thus to look after the problems of education of these weaker sections of the community; and the Ministry of Home Affairs has made it clear, time and again, that it looks forward to the Ministry of Education for guidance in all technical aspects of education and every now and then, references regarding special intricate problems in this sector are made to the Ministry.

The fourteenth function refers to the federal responsibility for strengthening national unity. One of the most important problems which faces the country at present is to strengthen the ties of national unity through programmes of emotional integration and to negate the fissiparous tendencies which have become so prominent, especially after the reorganization of States on a linguistic basis. This responsibility is so fundamental to the very existence of democracy and the defence of our freedom that it is hardly necessary to emphasise it. But unfortunately, very little is being done at present in this sector. The basic responsibilities in this programme will have to be that of the Government of India and the State Governments will have to cooperate whole-heartedly in their implementation. This is, therefore, an area where a good deal of fundamental thinking and intensive effort is immediately called for.

The fifteenth function is the provision of scholarships. One of the principal purposes underlying educational development is social justice and the provision of equality of educational opportunity for all. A liberal scheme of scholarships to help the talented and poor children thus becomes a very significant programme in educational reconstruction. Obviously, such a programme will have to be implemented jointly by the Government of India and the State Governments. The Federal Government admittedly has a special responsibility for the institution of scholarships at the University stage; but it is also argued that, unless an adequate provision for scholarships is made at the Secondary stage, poor and deserving children would never be able to qualify themselves for University admission. Both in the first and in the second Plans, very little has been done in this sector. It is, however, obvious that, for several years to come, this would be an important programme of educational reconstruction. The Government of India would have to play a leading part in its implementation by helping in the determination of right policies and by providing necessary financial assistance to State Governments.

The sixteenth function refers to advanced professional and vocational training. Under Entry 65(a) of the Seventh Schedule of the Constitution, the Federal Government is authorised to set up agencies and institutions for professional, vocational or technical training. Obviously, the State Governments are also competent to set up such institutions under Entry 11 of List II of the same schedule. It is, therefore, necessary to draw a dividing line between the Federal and State functions in this respect. If Entry 65(a) of List I is literally interpreted, it may be made to cover any course of professional, vocational or technical training from a tailoring class at one end to a post-graduate course for Plant Pathologists at the other. But obviously, this is not the intention of the Constitution. It should be assumed that the State Governments would make all the necessary provision for professional and vocational education; but there are advanced courses of professional and vocational education which are very costly and which could not possibly be maintained by every State. It is in this sector that the Government of India has a special role to play by providing such advanced courses as would be needed by the country in general or by more than one State in particular. Another objective for the organization of such courses would be to develop the highest type of professional and vocational education within the country itself and, to that extent, to reduce the necessity of sending students abroad for Higher education. For instance, it is not the responsibility of the Government of India to conduct an institution for pre-service training of teachers at the B.T. or B.Ed, level. It should rather concentrate itself on providing post-graduate courses of in-service training for higher grades of educational administrators and teacher educators.

The seventeenth function refers to the establishment of Union institutions and agencies for education. The federal government is required to establish and maintain educational institutions for a number of reasons. For instance, educational institutions have to be maintained for employees of the Central Government. They have also to be maintained in important commercial undertakings of the Government of India in order to meet the requirements of the population of the new towns which have been established for such undertakings. Military cantonments which are under the control of the Government of India are also required to maintain educational institutions, not only for defence personnel, but also for the general population living in cantonment areas. Apart from such special purposes, it is also the responsibility of the Centre to conduct educational institutions with two definite objectives: (1) to serve as experimental institutions in comparatively neglected or more significant fields; and (2) to cater to the needs of more than one State or for the country as a whole.

The eighteenth function refers to the provision of free and compulsory education to a l l children up to the age of 14 years as directed in Article 45 of the Constitution. If this Article is read with Article 12 of the Constitution, it will be evident that the provision of universal, free and compulsory Primary education is a joint responsibility of the Government of India, the State Governments and the local authorities. The role of the Government of India would obviously be restricted to the formulation of national targets to be reached, to the grant of financial assistance to State Governments for implementing this programme and to the maintenance of an equal standard of attainment, both in quantity and quality, in all parts of the country. The role of the State Governments would mainly be restricted to the provision of teachers, their training, and supervision. The local authorities will have to take responsibility for all the expenditure on the remaining items and will have to implement the programme satisfactorily with the help of grants-in-aid from the State Governments. Just as the grants-in-aid given by the Centre to the State Governments will have to be based on the principle of equalisation, the grants-in-aid given by the State Governments to the local authorities also will have to be passed on the same principle.

In other words, the grants-in-aid to richer local authorities would be proportionately less and those to the poorer local authorities would be proportionately greater.

The eighteen functions of the federal government in education discussed so far may be regarded as fairly non-controversial. The first four functions, as stated earlier, belong exclusively to the federal government and there can be no controversy about them. The remaining thirteen functions fall into the concurrent group. But it is universally agreed that the federal government has some responsibility with regard to each one of them, although there might be some slight difference of opinion regarding the extent arid nature of such role.

Over and above these seventeen functions, however, there are three other functions which are very important and which at present, have become highly controversial, viz. (i) the education of women, (ii) policy-making and (iii) financial assistance. It is therefore, necessary to discuss them in some detail. Education of Women.—The National Committee on Women's Education, it may be recalled, has recommended that the Government of India should assume a transitional special responsibility for this subject until the existing wide gap between the education of boys and girls is materially bridged. In the opinion of the Committee, women come under the expression "weaker section of the people" used in Article 46 of the Constitution. The Backward Classes Commission set up by the Government of India also recommended that women should be regarded as 'backward classes' and this strengthens the claim of treating their education as a responsibility of the Government of India under Article 46. The Committee has also put forward another strong argument in favour of its proposal. The Government of India admittedly has a special responsibility for providing free and compulsory education up to the age of 14. This responsibility is not being implemented at present mainly because the education of girls has lagged behind that of boys; and the Committee, therefore, claims that the responsibility of the Government of India under Article 45 cannot be fulfilled unless it also assumes some special responsibilities for the education of girls.

Those who do not accept this view argue that, under the proposal made by the Committee, education becomes almost a central subject. Since women form about half of the total population, the State Governments would be deprived of 50% of their responsibility if the education of girls becomes a special responsibility of the Centre; and if the other sectors for which the Government of India is also responsible are taken into consideration, the responsibilities of the Government of India would be far larger than those of the State Governments themselves. Secondly, it is also argued that it will not be possible for the Government of India to discharge this responsibility to any extent unless the willing and enthusiastic cooperation of the State Governments is obtained by making them constitutionally responsible for the programmes and providing them with the necessary financial assistance.

The only logical conclusion under these circumstances seems to be that the responsibility of the Government of India for the education of girls should cover, not the entire programme for the education of girls, but only the small quantum of a special programme which is needed to give it a fillip. Even the special programmes should not be directly implemented by the Centre. They should rather be included in the "Centrally sponsored" sector under which the programmes are planned by the State Governments on the lines of some general principles laid down by the Centre and also implemented by them through their own agencies. The provision for their expenditure, however, is made in the Central sector and the funds are made available to State Governments on a 100% basis, outside their plans and ceilings. If such a clear-cut policy is defined and adopted, even the States would welcome it; and it would obviously go a very long way in expediting the programmes of Women's education, particularly in the backward States.

Policy-making function.—The policy-making function of the Federal Government in education has now become one of the most controversial issues in education. Under entry 66 of List I the Government of India is required to coordinate and maintain standards in University education. Obviously therefore, it does get a right to make policy decisions in University education and these will be binding upon State Governments under Article 257(i) of the Constitution which lays down that the executive power of the State Government shall be so exercised as not to impede or prejudice the exercise of the executive power of the Union.

Should any State Government not accept these decisions, it would be open to the Government of India to take action under the same Article which also authorises the Union to give such directions to a State Government as may appear to be necessary for this purpose. But what about policy-making in Secondary or Primary education or in fields which are not specifically covered by Entries in List I of the Seventh Schedule? From the strictly legal point of view, it can be argued that the Government of India has no authority to make any policy decisions in these sectors and that even if it did make any policy decisions they cannot be enforced against the State Governments under Article 257(i) of the Constitution. Of course, it is possible to argue that the standards of University education are dependent on those in Secondary education and that the standards in Secondary education are, in their turn, dependent on those in Primary education and to deduce there from that the Government of India can also take policy decisions in the fields of Primary and Secondary education. Such an interpretation appears to be plausible; but one cannot say how the Courts would react to it if it is challenged.

At best, it appears to be a slippery position on which it would be dangerous to take a firm stand.

It is true that the Government of India has been taking decisions in all fields of education in the post-independence period and these decisions are mostly being accepted by State Governments. This result, however, is accidental and is due to two extraneous circumstances—

(1) the political fact that the same party is in power at the Centre and the States and (2) the financial fact that most of these decisions have been sugar-coated with liberal financial assistance. But it would be wrong to assume that this political situation will always continue and it would be equally difficult to justify the use of financial pressures for inducing States to accept policies to which they would not otherwise have agreed to. The present constitutional position, therefore, presents an impasse. On the one hand, education must be treated as a whole and it is neither possible nor desirable to break it up into two compartments— University education and other sectors. On the other hand, Government has only a limited authority for making policy decisions in the sector of University education while it is not at all empowered to take any policy decisions in other fields; and even if it were to take any such decision, it does not have the legal authority to enforce it against the State Governments.

What is the way out of this impasse? Three suggestions are being put forward and discussed in this context. The first and the most radical suggestion is to amend the Constitution and to make education a 'concurrent' subject. In support of this view, a number of weighty arguments are put forward and although some of these have been briefly referred to in the earlier discussion, it may still be desirable to sum up the whole case here. It is argued, for example, that the 'economic and social planning' for which the Union is primarily responsible cannot be attempted successfully unless the Centre is also empowered to plan education.

Secondly, it is claimed that educational policy is a national rather than a State or local concern and that, although the administration of education may be left to the States and local authorities, the major decisions of State policy must be taken by the Centre. Thirdly, it is pointed out that the Directive contained in Article 45 of the Constitution implies that the provision of free and compulsory education is a joint responsibility and that the Centre will not be in a position to play its role in this sector unless it has also the authority to take policy decisions in Primary education and to compel the State Governments, if necessary, to adopt them. Fourthly, it is pointed out that it is a fundamental responsibility of the Centre to maintain an equal standard of social services in all parts of the country and as education is the most significant of all social services, the Centre will have to provide an equality of educational opportunity for all children in the country. This can only be done if education is amenable to Central planning and control. Fifthly, it is pointed out that the educational leadership available in the States is often below par and, as no chain can be stronger than its weakest link, the Centre must often provide effective leadership from above—a function which can hardly be discharged satisfactorily unless it is empowered adequately to deal with recalcitrant cases; and finally, it is pointed out that the Centre is responsible to Parliament for all the funds it gives to State Governments for educational development and that it cannot really be answerable to Parliament in this behalf unless it also has the authority to take firm policy decisions and to implement them. The burden of the song is, therefore, clear; amend the Constitution and make education a concurrent subject. It must also be stated that there is a fairly large support for this view and in almost every Parliament session, the notice of a resolution to this effect is given by some member or the other.

As against this extreme view in one direction, there is a second group of thinkers who would prefer to go to an extreme in the other direction. They suggest that education is and should be a State subject and that the modern trend towards centralization must be resisted as forcefully as possible in the larger interests of the country. They demand decentralization in general—even in planning—on grounds of democracy and warn that centralization, which brings some immediate gains, is extremely harmful in the long run because it saps the selfconfidence, initiative, responsibility and even the competence of State Governments. In their view, a still greater need for decentralization in education is the possibility it affords to every linguistic minority to preserve its own culture and to progress in its own way. It is also argued that the varied mosaic pattern which Indian culture has evolved through centuries past can be preserved only if State Governments have real authority over education and that it can be destroyed in no time under a centralized control of education which would always tend to introduce dead uniformity. It is further urged that centralization of education would make it increasingly bureaucratic and thus deprive it of the healthy direct contact with the public. This group of thinkers, therefore, would not only preserve the sovereign authority which State Governments have over education at present, but they would even go a step further and cut at the very root of all trends of centralization by abolishing the Ministry of Education itself or by constituting a single small ministry for all social welfare services.

Between these two extreme views—one of which is close to Australia and the other to the U.S.S.R.—there is a third view which represents the latest thought on this subject in the U.S.A. and which may also be regarded as the 'golden mean' proposal of reform. According to this view, centralization of educational authority—and this is exactly what all the talk of making education a concurrent subject really means—is definitely harmful while a weak or inactive Centre is hardly better than cultural anarchy. What this group of thinkers recommends, therefore, is that the federal government should provide strong and competent leadership of a 'stimulating but non-coercive character'.

This leadership is to be provided in three ways—in ideas, in personnel, and in programmes.

1. The leadership in ideas is provided in two ways—through the development of research and through the coordinating and clearing house functions which cross fertilise educational thinking by making known the good work done in one area of the country to the remaining areas.

2. The leadership in personnel is generally provided in three ways—the maintenance of an advisory service, the training of educational administrators, and experimental work in the training of teachers. It is a fundamental responsibility of the Centre to scout for talent and to maintain an advisory

service of the best people available in the country and to make them available to State Governments for advice and assistance in all matters. Secondly, it is also a responsibility of the Centre to arrange for advanced professional training in educational administration and to provide for the in-service training of educational administrators through such programmes as seminars and workshops, special training or refresher courses, deputations for studies in the country or abroad, and production of necessary literature. Thirdly, the federal government has also a responsibility in the attempt to provide better teachers by advising and assisting the State Governments to adopt such measures as improving the remuneration and service conditions of teachers, conduct of experiments in teacher education, etc.

3. Finally, the leadership in programmes can be provided through the conduct of pilot or experimental projects.

It is claimed that if the Central Government can thus provide a competent professional leadership through ideas, men and programmes, the willing consent of the State Governments would be secured to whatever common policy the Federal Government desires to adopt and that such persuasion of the States is infinitely better than coercion under a constitutional authority. It is obvious that a conscious adoption of this policy is probably the best course to be followed in India.

Financial Assistance.—Then comes another of the most significant federal functions in education, viz., the provision of financial assistance for programmes of expansion and improvement of education. That the federal government must give such assistance is universally admitted; and the task is of special significance in India where the most elastic and productive sources of revenue are vested in the Centre. The main controversies, therefore, relate to two issues—the objectives of assistance and the form and conditions of grants-in-aid.

With regard to the first of these issues, it is generally suggested that there should be three types of grants. The first is a transfer of additional revenues in order to enable the State Governments to plan their programmes in all welfare services with greater confidence and self-reliance; the second is the institution of a general grant for educational purposes but not earmarked for any specific programme; and the third is a specific purpose grant which is intended for a programme organised and implemented with the approval of the Centre. It is obvious that if the autonomy and independence of the States is to be respected in the educational field, greater reliance will have to be placed on the first two of these grants. The mistake of the first Five-Year Plan was that innumerable specific purpose grants were created and they naturally led to a tremendous increase in administrative work and red tape. The mischief has been considerably undone in the second Five-Year Plan by introducing four main groups of grant-in-aid, by authorizing the States to reappropriate within the same group, and by introducing the system of ways and means advances. But even now, a good deal remains to be done and it would be worthwhile to simplify the system and to reduce the specific purpose grants still further during the Third Plan.

Another point of extreme importance is that of special financial assistance to backward States or what is called 'an equalization grant' in American parlance. As pointed out earlier, it is a basic responsibility of the federal government to maintain a uniform standard of social services in general and to equalise educational opportunities in particular. In this respect, our States show immense differences. They differ in the level of development reached at present due mainly to historical accidents; their 'educational loads' i.e. the number of children still outside the school also vary greatly; and even the social and economic conditions show equally wide variations so that the States are far from comparable in terms of 'ability' to support education and the difficulty of the task to be performed. The advanced States have a bigger and a more difficult task to perform with more limited resources. Today, the conditions are so diverse that the expenditure on Primary education in the single city of Bombay is greater than that in the entire State of Orissa. It is for the Government of India to adopt an equalization grant and level up such differences to the extent possible.

It should also be stated that it is not the object of the equalization programme to bring all developments to a dead level of uniformity. This need not and cannot be done. What is suggested is a three-fold programme: (1) the federal government should prescribe, from time to time, minimum or foundation programmes below which no area should be allowed to fall; (2) the freedom of individual States to go ahead should be retained; and (3) the gap between the advanced and the backward States should be continually narrowed down.

It is obvious that this principle of grant-in-aid is diametrically opposed to that of matching grants which gives more to him that hath. Under this concept, some States may get no grant, others may get a medium one and still others may get a large one. Its operation can probably be best described in the following passage from De Young:

"The Tenth Amendment to the Constitution of the United States made education the primary responsibility of the individual states. Hence the support of public education became mainly a matter of state concern. Today every state makes some contribution from its revenues for the support of public schools through many types of funds, some of which are described later. An inconsistency exists, however, between the legal intention to provide state support and the many cases of neglect and inadequacy.

For the nation as a whole, state governments supply only about 40 per cent of the cost of schools. Furthermore, the method of distributing such aid is an important factor. Despite favourable arguments for federal support of public education, the fact remains that the individual states will have to give more assistance to schools, particularly through the application of the next principle.

Strayer and Haig in 1923 were the first to give a clear-cut picture of the equalization principle. Their analysis interpreted this principle as the complete equalization of the burden of a satisfactory minimum educational programme below which no locality could be allowed to go, but above which any locality would be allowed to rise by means of local support. In contradistinction to the payment-for-effort or matching principle, the operation of the equalization plan tends to shift to more able communities some of the undue burden carried by the less wealthy localities (see Fig. below). Most states today have a state-local "partnership foundation programme" in which the commonwealth bestows more on these schools which have less in fiscal resources.

How state equalization works in three types of districts. In the poor district, local effort to support schools produces only a small fraction of the cost of a state-guaranteed minimum or foundation programme.

In the district of average wealth, the same effort produces about half the needed fiscal support. The wealthy district receives no state equalization aid because the local wealth back of each child is great enough to more than finance the minimum programme. The district serves as a lighthouse to indicate better practices.

In brief, the equalization principle means that governmental agencies collect educational funds where the money is and spend the money where the pupils are. Every man's property and income must be taxed to educate every man's child. Even though a man chooses to send his own children to a parochial or private school he is not exempt from contributing his support to the education of all children.

The golden rule in educational finance is : "Thou shalt educate thy neighbor's children as thine own."

At first this idea of equalization was applied to small areas, as the county and state. Now the old slogan "the wealth of the state must educate the children of the state" is being supplemented with the clause "and the wealth of the United States must be used to equalize the education of all the children in the nation". Furthermore, the phrase "all the children in the nation" implies that more adequate educational opportunities and greater financial support be provided for exceptional or a typical children, since their learning opportunities, as in the case of the blind, are below par, and the costs of their instruction are above average. American public education will not be genuinely democratic until there is nation-wide application of the principle that opportunity and burden shall be equalized for all learners."

The second issue refers to the conditions of grant-in-aid. Here strict adherence to certain general principles is necessary. To begin with, the tendency to use grants-in-aid as indirect pressure levers for policy decisions should be discouraged as far as possible. Secondly, the quantum of specific purpose grants should be restricted to the very minimum and confined to basic programmes of national significance only or schemes in the nature of experimental or pilot projects. Thirdly, the procedure for sanctioning these grants will have to be simplified to the utmost. And lastly, a suitable machinery will have to be devised to obtain, from the State Governments, a report on the utilization of grants and the results obtained thereof. This can probably be effectively done by appointing high level advisers who should pay visits to States and submit reports after a special study on the spot.

Another useful suggestion to be made in this context is that the specific purpose grants should be included in the Centrally-sponsored sector. In a Centrally-sponsored scheme, 'planning' should be a joint responsibility in which the fundamental principles are laid down by the

Centre, but a large initiative and freedom is left to State Governments to make the Plan suit its local needs and conditions; 'implementation' would be through the State Government; and 'finance' would come from the Centre on a hundred per cent basis and outside the State Plan and ceiling. This will ensure that the programme is most effectively implemented and also that such implementation does not interfere with any other schemes.

In this chapter, an attempt has been made to examine the various issues concerning the role of the Government of India in Education. The problem was approached from three angles, historically, constitutionally and comparatively from the point of the role which the federal governments of some of the foreign countries are playing in education.

In the historical survey which covered the period 1773—1950, it was shown that prior to 1833 the Centre had hardly any role to play; between 1833 and 1870 education was virtually a Central subject; between 1870 and 1921, while the day-to-day administration was vested in the provincial governments, the Government of India discharged five distinct functions, viz.,(1) policy-making, (2) serving as a clearinghouse for information, (3) promotion of research and publication of suitable literature, (4) coordination and (5) financial assistance; the years 1921-35 saw a virtual divorce between education and Central Government with disastrous consequences; but more progressive policies were evolved and the Government of India again began to play a more leading role.

In the next section, the Constitutional provisions relating to education were subjected to a close examination and it was shown that the present position is somewhat anomalous. On the one hand, the Constitution takes the simple stand that education, with all residuary powers, is a State subject; while in a number of important fields (such as the provision of educational facilities for children up to the age of 14, the promotion and safeguarding of the cultural interests of the minorities, the need for controlled development of Higher education etc.,) education appears to be more of a joint responsibility than an exclusive preserve of the States.

The study of the role of the federal government in education in certain other countries showed that the interest and activities of a federal government are not always guided by the provisions of the Constitution and that, in many instances, the federal government is taking a very definite and positive interest in the formulation and implementation of educational programmes even in the absence of any constitutional obligation for that purpose.

In the concluding section of the chapter, it was suggested that, without trespassing on the autonomy of the States, the Centre had a useful role to play in evolving suitable educational policies for the country and that in view of the greater elasticity of the Central tax structure it had a very definite responsibility for rendering financial assistance to the States towards the expansion and improvement of educational facilities.

BIBLIOGRAPHY

1. Association of Indian Universities (AIU) (1996) *Handbook of Engineering Education*, AIU, New Delhi.

2. Association of Indian Universities (AIU) (1999) *Directory of Universities and Colleges of India*, AIU, Reliance Publishing House, New Delhi.

3. Association of Indian Universities (AIU) (2002) *Universities Handbook (29th Edition)*, AIU, New Delhi.

4. Bhan, Sonja (2002) *India: The Private Sector Emerges in Higher Education*, World Education News & Reviews (WENR), New York.

5. Boston College Center for International Higher Education (2006) *International Higher Education*, published quarterly (journals), Massachusetts.

6. Bhushan, Sudhanshu and Anupama Bhatnagar (2005) *Country Paper – India*, Papers presented at eighth Session of the Regional Committee Meeting for the Regional Convention on the Recognition of Studies, Diplomas and Degrees in Higher Education in Asia and the Pacific.

7. Clark, Nick (2006), *Education in India*, WES – World Education News & Reviews (WENR), New York.

8. Department of Collegiate Education (2005) *Annual Administrative Report 2004-2005*, Government of Karnataka, Bangalore.

9.   Gnanam, A. (2002) *New Providers in Higher Education in India, Case study for UNESCO.*

10.   Government of Karnataka State (2001) *The Karnataka State Universities Act, 2000*, Bangalore.

11.   Government of Karnataka State (2006) *Report of the Taskforce on Higher Education – Shaping Education in Karnataka 2004*, Bangalore University Press, Bangalore.

12.   Ministry of Human Resource Development (1999) *Discussion Paper on Internationalization of Education, Department of Education*, Ministry of Human Resource Development, Government of India, New Delhi.

13.   National Assessment and Accreditation Council (NAAC) and Commissionerate of Collegiate Education of the Government of Karnataka (2003) *Total Quality Management for Tertiary Education*, NAAC, Bangalore.

14.   National Assessment and Accreditation Council (NAAC) (2004) *Quality Higher Education and Sustainable Development – NAAC Decennial Lectures 1994-2004*, NAAC, Bangalore.

15.   National Assessment and Accreditation Council (NAAC) (2004) Best Practices in Higher Education – Report of the National Conference Organized by NAAC, NAAC, Bangalore.

16.   National Assessment and Accreditation Council (NAAC) (2004), A Decade of Dedication to Quality Assurance, NAAC, Bangalore.

17. National Board of Accreditation (NBA) and All Indian Council for Technical Education (2004) Manual of Accreditation (Revised Edition, January – 2004), NBA, New Delhi.

18. National Council for Teacher Education (NCTE) (2004) Indian Journal of Teacher Education, Volume 1, Number 2, December, 2004, NCTE, New Delhi.

19. National Office of Overseas Skills Recognition (NOOSR) (1996) Country Education Profiles - India – A Comparative Study, (Second Edition), Department of Employment, Education and Training, Australian Government Publishing Service, Canberra.

20. National Office of Overseas Skills Recognition (NOOSR) (2005) Country Education Profiles - India – A Comparative Study, (Second Edition), Department of Employment, Education and Training, Australian Government Publishing Service, Canberra.

21. Patil, Jagannath (2006) Quality Assurance in Indian Higher Education, WES – World Education News & Reviews (WENR), New York.

22. Powar, K.B. (2001) (Ed.) Internationalization of Higher Education, Association of Indian Universities (AIU), New Delhi.

23. Sharma, Kavita A. (2003) 50 Years of University Grants Commission, University Grants Commission, New Delhi.

24. Singh, Sutinder (1995) Indian Universities-On the Upswing, World Education News & Reviews (WENR), Volume 8, Number 2, Spring 1995, New York.

25. Srikantewara, Sri K. & Dr. Siddalingaswamy (2004) Report of the Taskforce on Higher Education – Shaping Education in Karnataka, 2004, Government of Karnataka, Bangalore.

26. Stella, A (2001) Quality Assessment in Indian Higher Education: Issues of Impact and Future Perspectives, Allied Publishers, New Delhi.

27. Stella, A. and Gnanam, A. (2001) Assessment and Accreditation in Indian Higher Education: Issues of Policy and Prospects, Books Plus, New Delhi.

28. Stella, A. and Gnanam, A. (2002) Assuring Quality and Standards in Higher Education: The contemporary Context and Concerns. Allied Publishers, Bangalore.

29. Sweeney, Kallur, Smith, Maryak, Oliver and Stedman (1998) PIER World Education Services – India – Special Report 1997 (1998), AACRAO and NAFSA, Washington, DC.

30. University Grants Commission (UGC) (2002) X Plan of University Grants Commission, UGC, New Delhi.

31. University Grants Commission (UGC) (2004) Consolidating the Past and Strengthening the Future, UGC, New Delhi.

32. University Grants Commission (UGC) (2005) Annual Report 2003-2004 of the University Grants Commission, UGC, New Delhi.

33. University Grants Commission (UGC) (2005) List of Proposals for the Grant of Deemed University received and screened upto February 2005, UGC, New Delhi

APPENDIX 1

A list over statutory bodies which regulate the standards of education in various professional fields

Institution	Date of Establishment	Important Functions
University Grants Commission	UGC Act, 1956	Co-ordination and maintenance of standards of university education
National Accreditation and Assessment Council	Established in 1994 under 12cc of UGC Act, 1956	• To maintain standards of quality • Function of accrediting and assessing institutions of liberal arts, science and other disciplines • Recently teacher education institutions to be assessed • NAAC has accredited 2088 colleges and 113 Universities in India in 10 years since its establishment • Not obligatory
All India Council for Technical Education	AICTE Act, 1987	Planning, co-ordination, promotion of quality and maintenance of standards of technical education system in the country
National Board of Accreditation	Established in 1994 Under section 10(u) of AICTE Act, 1987	• To assess standards of quality of education • Assessing and accrediting institutions imparting technical education in India • Recommending body regarding recognition and de-recognition of institutions
National Council of Teacher Education	NCTE Act, 1987	• Statutory body to develop norms and standards of teacher education • Powers to give recognition to teacher education institutions offering various courses • Planned and co-coordinated development of teacher education institutions

Institution	Date of Establishment	Important Functions
Medical Council of India	Established in 1934, operational by new act in 1956	• Maintenance of uniform standards of medical education • Recommendation for recognition/de-recognition of medical qualification of medical institutions of India or foreign countries • Registration of doctors • Mutual recognition of medical qualifications of foreign countries
Dental Council of India (DCI)	1948	1. To regulating the Dental Education, Dental Profession, Dental ethics in the country 2. To recommend to the Government of India to accord permission to start a Dental College, start higher course and increase of seats in a college. 3. To inspect Dental Colleges and institutions.
Indian Nursing Council (INC)	1947	1. To regulate and maintain the uniform standard of training for Nurses, Midwives, Auxiliary Nurse-Midwives and Health Visitors. 2. The Council prescribes the syllabus and regulations for various nursing courses. 3. To inspect Nursing Schools and Examination Centers.
Council of Architecture (COA)	Architects Act 1972	1. To register Architects 2. To prescribe standards of education, recognition of Indian and foreign qualifications 3. To prescribe standards of practice to be complied with by the practising architects. 4. To regulate the standards of education and practice of profession throughout India besides maintaining the register of architects.
Bar Council of India (BCI)	1961	1. Empowered to make rules to discharge its functions under the Advocates Act 1961. 2. Rule-making power to laying down guidelines for the standards of professional conduct and etiquette to be observed by advocates. 3. To specify the conditions subject to which an advocate must have the right to practice and

Institution	Date of Establishment	Important Functions
		the circumstances under which a person must be deemed to practice as an advocate in a court. 4. To make rules regarding the duties that an advocate must perform in his interaction with colleagues in the profession. 5. It can only specify conditions that are applicable at the post-enrolment stage and not at pre-enrolment stage.
Pharmacy Council of India (PCI)	1948	1. To regulate the profession of pharmacy whereas it is expedient to make better provision for the regulation of the profession and practice of pharmacy. 2. To control Pharmacy education and profession in India up to graduate level.
Indian Council for Agriculture Research (ICAR)		1. To establish various research centers to meet the agricultural research and education needs of the country. 2. Activity involve in human resource development in the field of numerous agricultural universities spanning the entire country.
Rehabilitation Council of India (RCI)	1992	1. Prescribes that any one delivering services to people with disability, who does not possess qualifications recognized by RCI, could be prosecuted. 2. It has twin responsibility of standardizing and regulating the training of personnel and professional in the field of Rehabilitation and Special Education
Central Council of Homeopathy (CCH)	1973	1. To evolve uniform standards of education in Homoeopathy. 2. The registration of practitioners on the Central Register of Homoeopathy will ensure that medicine is not practiced by those who are not qualified in this system, and those who practice, observe a code of ethics in the profession
Central Council of Indian Medicine (CCIM)	1970	1. It prescribes minimum standards of education in Indian Systems of Medicine viz. Ayurved, Siddha, Unani Tibb. 2. It maintains a central register on Indian

Institution	Date of Establishment	Important Functions
		Medicine and prescribes standards of professional conduct, etiquette and code of ethics to be observed by the practitioners 3. It Provides and maintain the list of colleges recognized by the Council for education in Indian Systems of Medicine.
Veterinary Council of India	1984	1. To specify the minimum standards of veterinary education required for granting recognized veterinary qualifications by veterinary institutions 2. To recognize foreign veterinary qualifications
Distance Education Council	1991	To promote open university/distance education institutions, its coordinated development, and the determination of its standards.

179

UGC (Minimum Standards of Instruction for the Grant of the First Degree through Formal Education) Regulations

University Grants Commission New Delhi.

UGC (Minimum Standards of Instruction for the Grant of the First Degree through Formal Education) Regulations, 2003. *(In supersession of Notification No. F.1-117/83(CP) dated 25th November 1985, Notification No.F.1-117/83 (CPP) dated 30th May 1986 and Notification No.F.1-117/83 (CP) dated December 1998)*

In exercise of the powers conferred by clause (f) of sub-section (1) of Section 26 of the UGC Act 1956 (No. 3 of 1956), the University Grants Commission makes the following Regulations, namely:

SHORT TITLE, APPLICATION AND COMMENCEMENT

- These Regulations may be called the University Grants Commission (Minimum Standards of Instruction for the Grant of the First Degree through Formal Education) Regulations, 2003.

- These shall apply to all universities established or incorporated by or under a Central Act, a Provincial Act, or a State/Union Territory Act, and all institutions recognized by or affiliated to such Universities and all institutions deemed to be universities under Section 3 of the UGC Act 1956.

- These shall come into force from the date of their publication in the official Gazette.

- No student shall be eligible for admission to a first degree programme in any of the faculties unless he/she has successfully passed the examination conducted by a Board/University at the +2 level of schooling (either through formal schooling for 12 years, or through open school system) or its equivalent.

- The admission shall be made on merit on the basis of criteria notified by the university, keeping in view the guidelines/norms in this regard issued by the UGC and other statutory bodies concerned and taking into account the reservation policy issued by the government concerned from time to time.

- Student enrolment shall be in accordance with the academic and physical facilities available keeping in mind the norms regarding the student-teacher ratio, the teaching-non-teaching staff ratio, laboratory, library and such other facilities. The in-take capacity shall be determined at least six months in advance by the university/institution through its academic bodies in accordance with the guidelines/norms in this regard issued by the UGC and other statutory bodies concerned so that the same could be suitably incorporated in the admission brochure for the information of all concerned.

- Depending upon the academic and physical facilities available in the institutions, the university may allow an institution to admit a certain number of students directly to the second year of a first degree programme, if the student has either (a) successfully completed the first year of the same programme in another institution, or (b) already successfully completed a first degree programme and is desirous of and academically capable of pursuing another first degree programme in an allied subject.

TEACHER

- No person shall be appointed to a teaching post if he/she does not fulfil the minimum qualifications prescribed for recruitment as per the Regulations in this regard notified from time to time under Section 26 (1)(e) of the UGC Act 1956.

- Every teacher shall participate in teaching, which may include any or all of the following: lectures, tutorials, laboratory sessions, seminars, fieldwork, projects and other such activities.

- Every teacher shall also give general assistance to students in removing their academic difficulties; and participate in the invigilation and evaluation work connected with tests/examinations; and take part in extra-curricular, co-curricular and institutional support activities as required.

- The workload of a teacher shall take into account activities such as teaching, research and extension, preparation of lessons, evaluation of assignments and term papers, supervision of fieldwork as also guidance of project work done by the students. The time spent on extension work, if it forms an integral part of the prescribed course, shall count towards the teaching load. The total workload and the distribution of hours of workload for the various components shall be in accordance with the guidelines issued by the UGC and the other statutory bodies concerned in this regard from time to time.

WORKING DAYS

- Every university enrolling students for the first degree programme shall ensure that the number of actual teaching days on which classes such as lectures, tutorials, seminars, and practical's are held or conducted is not less than 180 in an academic year, excluding holidays, vacations, time set apart for completing admissions and time required for conduct of examinations.

- The timetable on working days shall be so drawn up that the physical facilities are adequately utilized and not used only for a few hours in a day.

- The total periods provided for contact teaching shall not be less than 30 hours a week.

- The time provided for practical's, field work, library, utilization of computer and such other facilities, and shall not be less than 10 hours a week.

SYLLABUS

- Depending upon the curricular pattern, whether the university follows the annual system, the semester system or the trimester system, the entire syllabus of the programme shall be divided into suitable courses spread evenly for the duration of the programme.

- The university shall endeavour to introduce a cafeteria approach by working out the division of the entire syllabus of the programme into courses in such a manner that a student can choose the number of courses according to his/her requirements.

- The university shall not only lay down the syllabus for each course, but also the manner of its implementation, namely, through lectures, tutorials, laboratory sessions, seminars, field work, projects and such other activities.

- Depending upon its nature and level, a course may be assigned a certain number of credits. The credits assigned to the various courses shall also be indicated in the respective syllabuses. The system of credits shall be in accordance with the guidelines of the UGC and other statutory bodies concerned.

- The syllabus for each course shall also indicate the scheme of evaluation/ examination.

- The students shall be encouraged to study some part of the syllabus themselves and shall be given assignments, so as to make use of the library, laboratory, internet and such other faculty.

- The total workload on a student shall also be adequate so as to provide him/her sufficient academic involvement.

- The minimum number of lectures, tutorials, seminars and practical's which a student shall be required to attend for eligibility to appear at the examination shall be prescribed by the university, which ordinarily shall not be less than 75% of the total number of lectures, tutorials, seminars, practical's, and any other prescribed requirements.

EXAMINATION AND EVALUATION

- The university shall adopt the guidelines issued by the UGC and other statutory bodies concerned from time to time in respect of conduct of 6.2 The units of evaluation, namely, tests, seminars, presentations, class performance, field work, and the like and the weight age assigned to each of such units in respect of each course shall be determined by the appropriate academic body of the university, and shall be made known to the students at the beginning of the academic session of the year, the semester or the trimester, as the case may be.

- The nature of final examination, whether written or oral or both, in respect of each course shall also be made known to the students at the beginning of the academic session.

- There shall be continuous sectional evaluation in each course in addition to trimester/semester/year-end examinations, and the weight age for seasonal evaluation and examination in respect of each course shall be prescribed by the appropriate academic body, and made known to the students at the beginning of the academic session.

- If the university follows grading system, it shall work out and adopt a table of conversion of grades into percentages and vice-versa.

- If the fieldwork or project work is prescribed as an integral part of a course, the weight age assigned to it should reflect the time spent on it.

- The question papers for the examinations shall be set in such a manner as to ensure that they cover the entire syllabus of the concerned course.

- The tests and examinations shall aim at evaluating not only the student's ability to recall information, which he/she had memorized, but also his/her understanding of the subject and ability to synthesize scattered bits of information into a meaningful whole. Some of the questions shall be analytical and invite original thinking or application of theory.

- While the actual process of evaluation shall be confidential, the system of evaluation shall be sufficiently transparent, and a student may be given a photocopy of his/her answer paper, if requested as per procedure laid down in this regard.

PHYSICAL FACILITIES

- Every university shall lay down the norms in respect of classrooms, laboratories, library, sports and health facilities, hostel accommodation, canteen/ cafeteria and such other facilities. All the institutions admitted to its privileges shall adhere to the same. While prescribing the norms for such facilities as a condition for affiliation, the university shall keep in view the guidelines/norms issued by the UGC and other statutory bodies concerned.

- The lecture classes shall normally have not more than 60 students, unless, in special cases, the institution has accommodation for larger classes and makes suitable audio-visual arrangements for effective lecturing accompanied by tutorial classes.

- For tutorials, a group shall not ordinarily be more than 20 students.

- For laboratory sessions, the size of a group shall depend upon the size of the laboratory, its type related to the specificity of the subject, the facilities available including the possibility or otherwise of controlling and supervising a number of students simultaneously through a central control panel, and such other devices. The ideal number of students for a normal laboratory session in subjects like Physics, Chemistry and Biology is 15. The number for Computer lab, Language lab, etc. may be higher or lower, depending upon the factors referred to above.

- The norms laid down by the concerned statutory body shall be followed in the case of laboratories in the professional courses.

AWARD OF DEGREES

- No student shall be eligible for the award of the first degree unless he/she has successfully completed a programme, of not less than three years duration and secured the minimum number of credits prescribed by the university for the award of the degree.

- The degree to be awarded may be called the bachelor?s degree in the respective discipline in accordance with nomenclature specified by the UGC under Section 22 (3) of the UGC Act.

INFORMATION

Every university shall furnish to the UGC information relating to the observance of the provisions of these Regulations in the form prescribed for the purpose. The information shall be supplied to the UGC within 60 days of the close of the academic year.

India	Norway
Completion of the first year of university education	Access to higher education
Bachelor Degree (3 years)	Recognized as equivalent to 120 ECTS credits at Bachelor degree level
Bachelor Degree (4 years)	Recognized as equivalent to Bachelor Degree / 180 ECTS credits
Bachelor of Education (1 year) before 1993	Not recognized as higher education
Bachelor of Education (1 year) 1993-1998	Recognized as equivalent to 30 ECTS credits at Bachelor Degree level
Bachelor of Education (1 year) 1999-now	Recognized as equivalent to 60 ECTS credits at Bachelor Degree level
Bachelor Degree (3 years) + Master Degree (2 years)	Recognized as equivalent to Bachelor Degree plus 60 ECTS credits at Master Degree level
Bachelor Degree (4 years) + Master Degree (2 years)	Recognized as equivalent to Bachelor Degree /180 ECTS credits plus Master Degree /120 ECTS credits, in total 5 years higher education / 300 ECTS credits
Bachelor Degree (3 years) + Master Degree (2 years) + Ph.D. (3years)	Recognized as equivalent to Bachelor Degree /180 ECTS credits plus Master Degree /120 ECTS credits plus 120 ECTS credits at Doctoral Degree level
Bachelor Degree (4 years) + Master Degree (2 years) + Ph.D. (3years)	Recognized as equivalent to Bachelor Degree /180 ECTS credits plus Master Degree /120 ECTS credits plus Ph.D. / 180 ECTS credits

DENMARK

India	Denmark
Higher/senior certificate (12 years of schooling) + 1 years of higher education	Access to higher education
Bachelor of Arts/Science/Commerce (pass) /3 years	2 years of Danish Bachelor Degree
Bachelor of Arts/Science/Commerce (honours) /3 years	2 years of Danish Bachelor Degree, eventually Danish Bachelor Degree
Bachelor of engineering/4 years	Danish Bachelor Degree or Danish Professional Bachelor Degree within engineering
Master of Arts/Science/Commerce /1 to 2 years	4 years of Danish Candidatus Degree, eventually a Danish Candidatus Degree in case of a written thesis
Master of Engineering /2 years	Danish Candidatus Degree
Postgraduate Diploma (PGD) /1 to 2 years	Danish Diploma or Master Degree if program is recognized by AICTE
Master of Philosophy	Individual assessment
Ph.D / 3 years	Danish Ph.D. Degree
Denmark is considering giving access to higher education to applicants having a higher/senior Secondary Education certificate (12 years of schooling) from CBSE and CISCE with a result of minimum 65%. This is due to the general recognition of the quality of the curriculum and examination organized by the two boards.	

SWEDEN

India	Sweden
3-Year Bachelor Degree	högskoleexamen
4-Year professional degree	kandidatexamen
4-Year engineering degree	högskoleingeniörexamen

Master's Degree	Kandidatexamen or magisterexamen med ämnesdjup
Master of Philosophy	No natural counterpart
Doctor Degree	doktorexamen

Some problems that might arise when evaluating the Indian degrees in the Swedish context is that the structure differs between the education systems in the two countries so that an Indian bachelor degree might cover many different subjects. Another problem is that the second bachelor degree, such as the Bachelor of Education, does not necessarily make any difference in the evaluation statement. This happens when the first degree is compared to a högskoleexamen. Then an extra year does not add enough depth in one subject to make it possible to change to comparison to a kandidatexamen.

APPENDIX 4

GROSS ENROLMENT RATIO (GER) FOR HIGHER EDUCATION

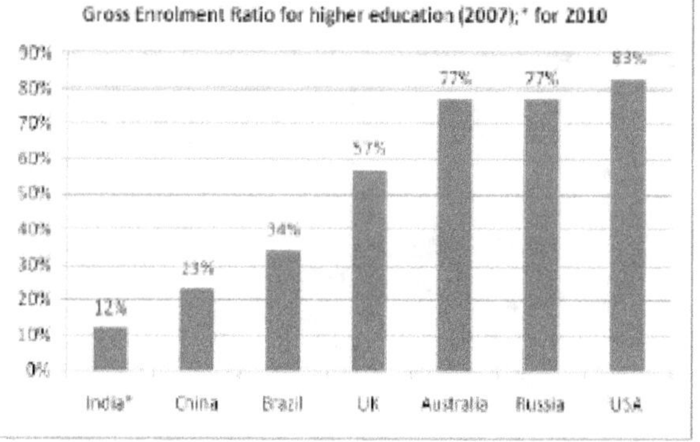

Source: Chinaeducenter.com, UNESCO Global Education Digest 2009; EY Analysis

191

CAPACITY UTILIZATION

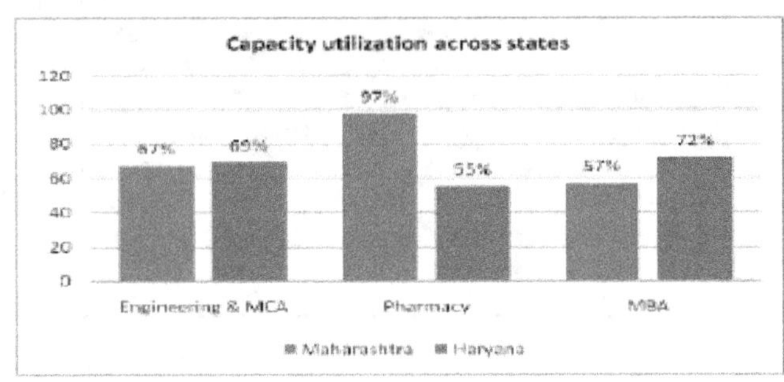

Source: Maharashtra DTE, AITCE; EY Analysis

APPENDIX 6

STUDENT TEACHER RATIO (2008)

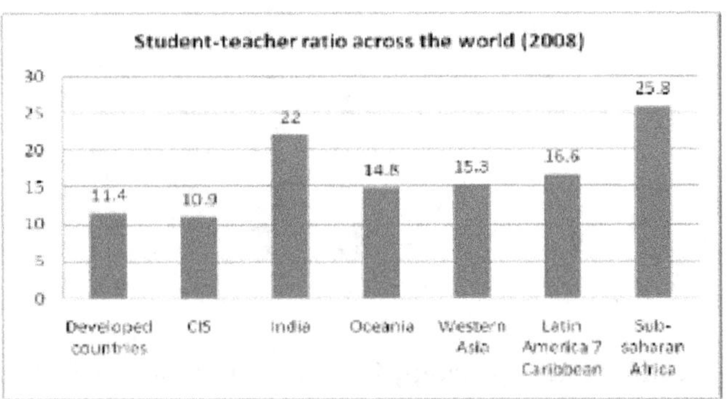

Source:"Higher Education in India", UGC Report, 2008; UNESCO Institute for Statistics 2010; EY Analysis